CHASING GOLD
Sportswomen of Ireland

CHASING GOLD

Sportswomen of Ireland

Yvonne Judge

WOLFHOUND PRESS

First published 1995 by
WOLFHOUND PRESS Ltd
68 Mountjoy Square
Dublin 1

British Library Cataloguing in Publication Data
A catalogue record for this book is available from the British Library

ISBN 0-86327-447-1

Typesetting: Wolfhound Press
Printed in Ireland by Colour Books, Dublin.
Cover photographs: Courtesy of Inpho.
Cover design: Joe Gervin.

Photographs in the colour section: courtesy of Inpho except photographs of Caroline Barker (by Liam Healy), Angela Farrell and the *Maiden* (courtesy of Angela Farrell) and final photograph of Michelle Smith (Popperfoto). Also black and white photographs on pages 51, 96, 98, 101, 143 courtesy of Inpho. On pages 23, 25 courtesy of Angela Farrell. On pages 73 courtesy of Rosemary Smith and bottom page 73 Frank Fennell. On pages 13, 31, 35, 44, 45, 63, 65 courtesy of *The Irish Press*. Photograph on page 80 courtesy of John Sheehan. Photographs on page 123 courtesy of Caroline Norris. On page 136, 137 courtesy of Popperfoto. On pages 139 courtesy of Sportsfile. Photographs on page 147 by Austin Finn, courtesy of *The Irish Press*. Photograph on page 149 by Russell Banks, courtesy of *The Irish Press*.

Contents

Acknowledgements

I would like to thank the following people for their invaluable help to me while writing this book:

Firstly the eleven sportswomen themselves who tolerated me popping up at the most inopportune moments in their pressurised lives and for their invaluable co-operation. Also, to the many people associated with them, who gave freely of their opinions and help.

Siobhan Campbell, Seamus Cashman and Susan Houlden of Wolfhound Press for their expert advice, assistance and, of course, patience. My former colleagues in The Irish Press, particularly John Redmond and Martin Brehany for their support and advice. Also to all my other colleagues on the sports desk and in the other editorial areas. The Irish Press and RTE.

I am indebted to the photo library of The Irish Press, Pearse Street Library and The National Library. My family, friends and flatmates for support and tolerance, and my sister Valerie for her administrative expertise. And also the following without whom I could not have completed this book: Kathryn Davis, Carol Flynn, Phil Minshull, Frank Greally, Padraig Slattery, John Saunders, Julian Davis, Terry Prone, Frank Quinn, Dr Maura O'Brien, Dr Mary Kelly, Dr Pat O'Neill, Eamon Coghlan, John Treacy, Joe Doonan, Sean Kennedy, Peadar McKiernan, John O'Sullivan, Pat Duffy, Brídin Ní Mhaolagain, Joan Priestman, Eamon Cregan, Brian Smith. An Cumann Camógaíochta, The Irish Ladies Hockey Union, The Irish Amateur Swimming Association.

If I have omitted to thank anyone,
mea culpa.

Yvonne Judge

Preface

When Wolfhound Press initially approached me to discuss writing this book, I hesitated briefly for fear that such a publication would be regarded as 'tokenism'.

However, it quickly became apparent that there was a need for such a book — that in the last century, and particularly in the last three decades, Ireland has produced some remarkable sportswomen. This book, however, is not a publication on sports which are exclusive to women, it is a book on eleven remarkable Irish people who are outstanding in their sports and who happen to be women.

Some are better known than others. The names of Sonia O'Sullivan, Catherina McKiernan and Michelle Smith trip readily off the tongue. Others are pioneering figures — Mary McKenna and Rosemary Smith. In Gaelic Games, the Downey sisters are known in all quarters and in the equine world Ann-Marie O'Brien and Caroline Hutchinson have made their mark. Then there is the youth of Karen Nugent and the world-beating prowess of Angela Farrell and Sandra O'Gorman.

In organisational terms, the hosting of the eighth women's hockey world cup is a case study for any ambitious sporting body, and the two closing chapters focus on the close relations to sporting success: health and money.

Finally, nobody is claiming that the women in this book are the greatest Irish sportswomen ever to the exclusion of all others. They are not necessarily the best eleven, but they are certainly eleven of the best.

Yvonne Judge

Backward Glimpses

These rules must be observed also in athletics and gymnastic exercises where special precaution must be taken in regard to Christian modesty in the case of girls, inasmuch as it is extremely unbecoming for them to display themselves before the public gaze. *Pope Pius XI, Divini Illius Magistri, 1929.*

In the sixty-five years since Pope Pius XI issued the encyclical letter containing the above passage, women's sport has come a long way, and Irish women's sport more than most.

For thirty-one years modesty denied many Irish women the chance to try their skills at athletics and other sports. From 1934 to 1965, the National Association for Cycling and Athletics in Ireland (NACAI), the governing body for those sports on this island then, did not run any national championships for women in athletic events. Today, only thirty years since women were allowed to compete on a national level in athletics, it is amazing how far they have come: two European gold medals and one world silver medal won in 1994 by two women: Catherina McKiernan and Sonia O'Sullivan, and a silver and gold world medal in 1995.

The reasons for this huge gap in time have much to do with the thinking displayed in the opening quote of this chapter. In an editorial of 4 May 1928, *The Irish Times* had this to say about the Pope's encyclical:

In France, Germany and even in England, many girls are devoting themselves to public sports which demand violent exertion and sometimes, it would seem, a notable scantiness in clothing.... These performances are done before crowds of male spectators. His holiness is surely in the right when he says that they are 'irreconcilable with women's reserve'.

It may seem laughable these days that this concern for modesty cut short many promising athletic careers, but it is worth noting that both women's hockey and camogie survived this century without interruption only because of the gymslip. Things were not always that grim, however.

The Irish Ladies Hockey Union made the first foray by Irish women into international sporting competition. The association was founded in 1894 (a year before its English counterpart), and two years later the first women's international hockey match took place at Old Alexandra, Milltown in Dublin, when Ireland defeated England 2-0. The ILHU remains today the oldest hockey union in the world.

An Cumann Camógaíochta was established in 1904. The forward-thinking Sean O'Duffy, working through the Gaelic League, set up the association with the belief that 'something should be done for the ladies'.

In 1893, the Irish Ladies Golf Union was formed, two years after the first open ladies' golf competition was held in Ireland. In 1907 the Irish ladies' golf team won the first-ever home internationals tournament in Newcastle, an achievement they did not repeat until 1980. (In light of such a fine history, it seems extraordinary that some Irish golf clubs continue to exclude women members over a century later.)

Irish women made their Olympian debut in Paris in 1924, when a certain Miss Willis and Mrs Phoebe Blair-White represented Ireland at tennis, although they competed under the Union Jack. Four years later women were admitted to compete in a limited number of 'non-traditional' events at the Amsterdam Olympics. While no Irish women participated in the track and field events, we did have a female representative, a Miss M. Dockrell, at the swimming pool, which you think would have generated a stir regarding modesty. Yet the example of emancipation clearly had an effect on the Irish sporting populus. In the 1929 Civil Service Sports, Miss H. Nolan of the Revenue Commissioners beat Miss M. Barrett of the Post Office in the 100 yards dash by a distance of three yards, after starting with the benefit of a twelve-yard handicap. Miss Barrett recovered from the distress of losing to an obviously ill-judged handicap, however, and went on to win the 100 yards championship of Ireland over Miss V. Cummins and Miss J. Baird at Croke Park.

There still were no official national athletic championships for women, however, and the shadow of clerical disapproval hung over the subject. The 1932 Olympic team had no women members, though the nation was happily distracted by the heroic gold medal of Bob Tisdall and the retention of Dr Pat O'Callaghan's Olympic crown.

In 1934, the NACAI held its annual congress. A motion was put before the body that the association should hold national championships for women in 100 yards, 440 yards, 80 yards hurdles and long jump, to be held in conjunction with the National Track and Field Championships. A lengthy debate ensued. Mr Padraig O'Keefe, General Secretary of the GAA, said that he had received complaints about women running in Croke Park. Mr O'Reilly of Ulsterville remarked that women's athletics had been taking place for some time in Ulster, although the GAA in Antrim had complained about the appearance of women in anything other than 'gym dresses'. On the other hand, the chairman remarked that the NACAI was the most backward international association in respect of women's athletics. The motion was passed, with a rider stipulating that the events be held separate from the National Championships for the sake of modesty.

Two days later, a letter was published in *The Irish Times* of 7 February 1934 from the president of Blackrock College, the Very Rev. John Charles McQuaide.

> Sir, - I have noted in yesterday's press a majority decision of the annual congress of the NACAI in favour of women competing in the same athletic meetings as men.

I protest against this un-Catholic and un-Irish decision.

I hereby assure you that no boy from my college will take part in any athletic meeting controlled by your organisation at which women will compete, no matter what attire they adopt.

The letter prompted much debate within the NACAI, and after another meeting on March 10 the matter was shelved until the following year. It was in fact not heard of again until 1947, thirteen years later.

No NACAI athlete participated in the 1936 Olympics in Berlin, due to their exclusion from the International Amateur Athletics Federation. Because of the Second World War, the Olympics were suspended for twelve years, and the next opportunity for international representation was in London in 1948. (However, there was to be no athletic representation for Ireland at the London Olympics, and the only woman member of the Irish team was Dorothy 'Tommy' Dermody, a fencer.)

In 1947 Crusaders Athletic Club in Dublin considered the formation of a ladies' section. In 1948 the club held a meeting at Lansdowne Road in Dublin featuring women's events: a few sprints and the high jump. The matter was put before an extraordinary general meeting in 1949. The motion was passed, and the ladies' section was formally ratified. However, what in other circumstances may have thrived was stunted by another disapproving interjection, this time from the Archbishop of Dublin, Dr John Charles McQuaide.

In his 1950 Pastoral Letter to the Diocese of Dublin, which was read in every Roman Catholic Dublin church on February 27, the archbishop commented:

We take the occasion to express our grave disapproval of the practice which has begun to show itself of permitting young women to compete in cycling and athletics in mixed public sports.

Although no law had been passed, nor any grander retribution threatened, the pastoral letter did its work. Ireland in the late forties did not need legal prohibition of an activity to stultify its growth; ecclesiastical disapproval was enough.

In 1951, after four years of relative inactivity, the ladies' section of Crusaders was formally disbanded. Amazingly, it would be another decade before the section was revived.

Sport did not come to an end for women in Ireland, however. Hockey and camogie continued to thrive, with Kathleen Mills and Sophie Brack prominent with sliothar and stick in the forties. Irish hockey in the thirties boasted the splendid legend of a woman known to all simply as 'Mrs Charters', who won thirty-eight caps for Ireland, a record which held until Johnny Lambert came along in the following decade. In 1948 Iris Kellett became the first woman to win an individual equestrian class at the Royal Dublin Society, and the following year she won the Queen Elizabeth Cup for showjumping at White City in London.

Notably however, athletics was not off limits for all Irish women. In Ulster the sport took off with great enthusiasm after the 1948 Olympics. Fanny Blankers-Koen followed her thrilling four golds at the London Games with visits to Belfast and Dublin, sparking an interest in athletics which was stifled in the South. When a West Indian women's sprinting team arrived in Belfast, local opposition was quickly rounded up. This group evolved into the 'Shorts and Harlands Athletics Club', the first such club in Ireland which accepted women members.

In 1949, as a direct result of these happenings, the North of Ireland held its first Irish Women's Athletics Championships. More importantly, and with remarkable foresight, Dutch coach Franz Stampfl was hired to promote athletics in the province. While the South sat in limbo, the Dutchman trawled the talent of the province and produced one of the greats: Thelma Hopkins.

Hopkins played hockey for Ireland, but her athletics career came under the Union Jack. She excelled at the long jump and high jump. At the age of sixteen, she qualified for the 1952 Helsinki Olympics and came fourth in the high jump. Ireland had one female representative at Helsinki: equestrian Emily Little.

At the 1948 Crusaders meeting in Lansdowne Road, Maeve Kyle, a hockey teammate of Thelma Hopkins, ran in the sprint. Kyle married and moved to Ballymena in 1955, which enabled her to participate in the Northern Championships. She won the sprint title there, and by this ironic turn in fortunes was chosen by the Olympic Council of Ireland to participate at the Melbourne Olympics of 1956 in the 100 and 200 yards.

It was a big year: Ronnie Delaney's gold, Fred Tiedt's silver, Johnny Caldwell's bronze, Maeve Kyle's debut, and Thelma Hopkins' silver in the high jump for Britain.

Kyle appeared in two more Olympic Games and earned no less than forty-five hockey caps for Ireland. Alongside Maeve Kyle on the hockey pitch, Joan Priestman won only two fewer international caps than her friend; forty-three. And in camogie, Una O'Connor blazed a trail for the sport from 1953 to 1966 with thirteen All-Ireland medals.

The 1960 Olympics in Rome featured Kyle again in athletics, and Shirley Armstrong represented Ireland in fencing's foil event. In Tokyo in 1964, Kyle was again the lone Irish woman, running in the 400 and 800 yards, but four years later in Mexico there was significant Irish female representation (though not in athletics).

The sixties saw women's athletics awake from its unofficial administrative slumber in the South of Ireland, and presumably the success of Maeve Kyle had a lot to do with that. The Crusaders revived its interest of a decade previously and moved to resurrect the ladies' section of the club, and in January 1962 the proposal for the establishment of a women's section of the club was unanimously passed.

In 1963 ladies' events were included in an international meet against

Left: Mary Peters of Belfast wins the gold in the Heptathlon, Munich, Olympics, 1972.

Belgium and Scotland in Brussels. Most of the women who competed for Ireland that day were from the North, including a talented young woman from Belfast named Mary Peters. Billy Morton was the manager of that history-making cross-border team, which succeeded in defeating both Scotland and Belgium.

In October 1963 Clonliffe Harriers followed the example of their Dublin rivals and formed a ladies' section. Officially, the NACAI still had no provision for holding ladies' events, but gradually momentum was building around the country. On 11 April 1965, the NACAI congress considered the following motion: That the NACAI actively encourage ladies' athletics in Ireland. The motion was adopted and history was made. Women's athletics once again formally existed in Ireland.

In March 1967 an Irish women's team competed at the inaugural Women's International Cross-country Championships in Wales, where they finished in second place behind the English team.

Meanwhile, an Irish woman was making her mark internationally in golf: Philomena Garvey. Ms Garvey won the Irish national title fifteen times and in 1964 was the first Irish woman to turn professional.

Such emancipation came a little early for the Mexico Olympics. With Maeve Kyle retired, Ireland had no official athletics representatives at the Games. Belfast's Mary Peters did compete, but her performance was severely hampered by injury.

The Irish team did, however, have its largest contingent of women to that point: two swimmers and five members of the equestrian team. Ann O'Connor and Vivienne 'Vicki' Smith flew the aquatic flag in the 100 and 200 yards breaststroke and butterfly respectively, and the equestrian team was boosted by Diane Connolly-Carew, Ada Matheson, Penny Moreton, Diana Wilson and Juliet Jobling-Purser. The sport of equestrianism has long had a healthy representation of women in Ireland, and 1968 was the first of many good Olympic teams boasting their presence.

Olympic success was mirrored when Iris Kellett won the European Ladies Title on Morning Light in 1968. And that wasn't all. Throughout Ireland and all over the roads of Europe, a tall blonde young woman with nerves of steel named Rosemary Smith was rallying her way into the history books, and a young woman named Mary Purcell was beginning to be impressive on the track.

The last reminder of the problem of modesty cropped up in 1971, when the Ladies' Intervarsity Cross-country Championship was held separately from the men's competition as the dressing rooms of Maynooth were thought to be inadequate. The concern was not over the comfort of the women, but fear of showing flesh to those who should not see.

The Olympic Games in Munich in 1972 had the largest representation of female athletes ever seen on an Irish team. There were three track athletes: Claire Walsh, Margaret Murphy and Mary Tracey (Purcell); and no less than four competing in swimming: Ann O'Connor, Aisling O'Leary, Christine Fulcher and Brenda McGrory. These four were the first (and only) Irish women to compete as a team in the 4 x 100 metres relay in both freestyle and the medley. Since then, Ireland has not had enough competitors in swimming, either male or female, to enter the team relay events. Juliet Jobling-Purser competed in equestrian events, and, another first, Ann McQuaid paddled in the K1 individual canoeing sprint.

Munich will forever be known to Irish sports fans as the year Mary Peters won the gold medal in the women's modern pentathlon. At thirty-two, the veteran Peters was rank outsider in the event, but she proved the pundits and suspicious officials wrong (their request for her to take a gender test was the first in the history of Olympic competition).

The seventies also saw Irish women making strides outside the Olympics: 1972 was the year of fifteen-year-old Angela Downey's first All-Ireland final in camogie for Kilkenny. Her sister Ann had her first taste of the Croke Park atmosphere two years later. In 1973 a breakthrough was made into the male bastion of football when the Ladies Football Association of Ireland was formed from the base of clubs in the civil service and around the country. The association grew to have 5,000 registered players in 1994. In 1979 Hermitage Golf Club in Dublin was the venue for the Irish women's amateur golf team's victory in the European Championships. The home crowd was thrilled to witness one of the most famous international golfing wins for Ireland.

Mary Purcell was back in the Montreal Olympics in 1976, this time in the 1500 metres. Purcell acquitted herself well by finishing fifth in her heat. Swimming again proved to be a strong event for Irish women, and Miriam Hopkins-Chambers and Deirdre Sheehan competed in the butterfly and freestyle events.

The American boycott of the Moscow Olympics stole the headlines in 1980, but the Irish team had three female representatives: Catherine Bohan in swimming, and representatives of two new sports: Hazel Greene-Perreira in archery and Frances Cryan in single sculls rowing.

In 1983 hockey and golf again took the international honours. The Irish women's hockey team won the Intercontinental Cup in Kuala Lumpur, and the Irish ladies won their second European title at Waterloo in Belgium. Ladies' cricket in Ireland underwent something of a revival in the eighties; after its foundation in the thirties, the sport had gone into decline. Clarissa Pilkington and Isolde Howard were instrumental in the sport's revival.

The Los Angeles Olympics of 1986 had Ireland's largest-ever representation of women athletes, fourteen in all. In archery, Hazel Greene had a companion in Mary Vaughan, and in swimming, Julie Parkes and Carol-Anne Heavey competed in the butterfly and freestyle. The equestrian team once again had a good female representation in Sarah Gordon, Margaret Tolerton and Fiona Wentges, but athletics stole the show: Monica Joyce and Róisín Smith in the 3000 metres; Carey May and Regina Joyce in the marathon; Mary Parr in the 400 metres hurdles; and Patricia Walsh in the discus. The star of the Moscow show, apart from the medal- winning boxers and Eamon Coghlan, who finished fourth in the 1500 metres, was Caroline O'Shea in the 800 metres, who became the first Irish woman to reach an Olympic athletics final.

At Seoul in 1988 Hazel Greene-Pereira completed her hat trick of Olympic appearances. Two yachtswomen debuted in the same Games; Cathy McAleavey and Aisling Byrne sailed together in the women's 470 class to finish twelfth. Ann Keenan-Buckley, Marie Murphy-Rolling, Ailis Smith and Barbara Johnson competed in athletics, and Ireland had two female swimmers: Aileen Convery and a seventeen-year-old Dublin girl named Michelle Smith.

At the 1990 European Championships in Split, Yugoslavia, the young Cork athlete Sonia O'Sullivan qualified for the final of the 800 metres. The following year O'Sullivan broke the world record for the indoor 5000 metres at the Boston Armory Track in the USA. In 1992 Catherina McKiernan won the silver medal in the World Cross-country Championships in Boston, with O'Sullivan finishing in seventh place. That summer, McKiernan and O'Sullivan represented Ireland in the Barcelona Olympics. O'Sullivan qualified for the final of the 3000 metres and finished fourth. McKiernan failed to match her cross-country achievement and finished eighth in her heat of the

3000 metres. Perri Williams was the first Irish woman to compete in the walk.

Michelle Smith carried the Irish tricolour into the stadium in Barcelona and competed in the individual medley and backstroke. Her day, however, was yet to come.

In 1993 the World Cross-country Championships were held in Bilbao, Spain. Sonia O'Sullivan did not compete as she was injured, but Catherina McKiernan performed brilliantly on the fast surface to take the silver medal again. In the same year, the World Athletics Championships were held in Stuttgart, and after her phenomenal run of Grand Prix successes, O'Sullivan was favourite to take the 3000 metres gold medal. The new Chinese athletes stole her thunder, however, and she finished fourth. She came back in the 1500 metres to win a very popular silver medal.

In December 1993 seventeen-year-old Karen Nugent was invited to play in the second annual TSB Women's Tennis Classic in Dublin. Nugent played and lost without losing face to Martina Navratilova in the RDS.

If there was a year in Irish sporting history that could be called the Year of the Women, it was 1994. McKiernan won silver in the World Cross-country Championships and a gold in the inaugural European equivalent; and O'Sullivan took gold in the European Athletics Championships, a first for any Irish athlete. The eighth Women's Hockey World Cup was held in Dublin, and Irish goalkeeper Sandra O'Gorman won the award for goalkeeper of the tournament. Irish swimmer Michelle Smith realised her potential, and after winning two medals in the short course World Cup meets early in the year became the first Irish swimmer to reach a World Championships final in Rome, where she finished in fifth place. Finally, the Ladies Irish Holidays Golf Open in Dublin attracted Laura Davies and other top names in international women's pro golf to Ireland.

This banner year ended with the first-ever National Forum for Women's Sport in Ireland, held in December in Dublin Castle. If they thought that the achievements of 1994 could not be bettered, then they were wrong. Catherina McKiernan won yet another silver medal in the 1995 World Cross-country Championships, and in August, Sonia O'Sullivan became the first Irish woman to win a gold medal at the World Athletics Championships in Gothenburg in the 5000 metres. Two weeks later, Michelle Smith followed up in the swimming by winning a silver and gold at the European Championships in Vienna. It was sixty years since John Charles McQuaide had withdrawn the boys of Blackrock from competition with female athletes over the question of modesty. These days, neither attire nor achievements in Irish women's sport can be called immodest. Great advancements and achievements have been made, but the best is probably yet to come.

Angela Farrell

Angela Farrell of Dalkey, county Dublin, was a member of the first all-woman crew to sail around the world when she took part in the 1989 Whitbread Round the World race as one of the crew of the *Maiden*. Angela was introduced to the joys of sailing at an early age, sailing on the Shannon estuary every summer and joining the rest of the Farrell clan on an expedition to France on a 38-foot yacht at the age of eight. She flew on an airplane for the first time at eighteen. As a teenager she sailed dinghies, started crewing on bigger yachts, and competed in the Irish Series of Offshore Races. Her five siblings are also sailing fanatics, and one of her sisters was sailing in the Arctic when Angela set off on the Whitbread. Angela lives in Dalkey with her husband, Brendan, and their son, Shane.

The **Whitbread** Round the World Race 1989

Leg 1. — Start 2 Sept. '89 Arrive Punta Del Este 9-18 Oct.
Leg 2. — Start 28 Oct. Arrive Fremantle 29 Nov.-10 Dec.
Leg 3. — Start 23 Dec. Arrive Auckland 12-16 Jan. '90.
Leg 4. — Start 4 Feb. Arrive Punta Del Este 28 Feb.-8 Mar.
Leg 5. — Start 17 Mar. Arrive Fort Lauderdale 13-21 Apr.
Leg 6. — Start 5 May Arrive Southampton 21-29 May.

Leg. 1 — Solent — Punta Del Este — 6,281 nautical miles
Leg. 2 — Punta del Este — Fremantle — 7,650 nautical miles
Leg. 3 — Fremantle — Auckland — 3,434 nautical miles
Leg. 4 — Auckland — Punta del Este — 6,255 nautical miles
Leg. 5 — Punta del Este — Fort Lauderdale — 5,475 nautical miles
Leg. 6 — Fort Lauderdale — Solent — 3,837 nautical miles

TOTAL DISTANCE: 32,932 nautical miles.

The Crew

Tracy Edwards, skipper and navigator, English, age 27
Angela Farrell, sail trimmer, Irish, age 26
Claire Russell, doctor, English, age 27
Michelle Paret, watch leader, French, age 35
Mikaela Van Koskull, helmswoman, Finnish, age 31

Mandy Swan, rigger, New Zealand, age 25
Jo Gooding, cook, Welsh, age 26
Jeni Mundy, electronics, English, age 24
Dawn Riley, watch leader, American, age 25
Nancy Hill, sail trimmer, English, age 27
Sally Creaser, mast, Scottish, age 28
Tanja Visser, foredeck, Dutch, age 27

*'I have never been that committed to anything in my life before. Never.
No competition. No thing. No people.'*

The Whitbread Round the World race is the ultimate sailing challenge —
two years of sailing over six legs, with two transatlantic runs, the rounding of
Capes Horn and Good Hope, and two legs through the dreaded Southern
Ocean. To say it is a journey of hardship and danger is an understatement. Five
people went overboard during the Whitbread that year, one of whom did not
survive. Another sailor died in a car crash, and the Russian crew captain
committed suicide. Such is the pressure of the Whitbread, a race which asks
the ultimate in team commitment and co-operation.

When Tracy Edwards decided to gather an all-woman crew for the 1989
Whitbread race, most people said she was mad. When she began her quest in
1988, Angela Farrell was working as an insurance clerk. If anyone had
suggested to Angela that within twelve months she would be living on a yacht
with ten other women as they travelled around the world, she would have said
he was mad. But a chance meeting with Tracy Edwards in a yacht club bar in
Cork lead to a berth on the *Maiden*, and a trip round the world the hard way.

Contrary to rumour, Angela was not recruited to replace the Frenchwoman
Marie-Claude, but as a replacement for an engineer who did not have enough
experience of offshore sailing. On this point of experience Angela is
disarmingly modest, but her success at lasting the pace speaks for itself more
than any accolade. There may have been technically better women sailors in
Ireland, but on the Whitbread sailing requirements is only the half of it; an
awful lot depends on how the crew works together.

And what of the crew? For Angela, they are now like sisters to her. She
grew up with them. She had joined the *Maiden* for the earlier, Fastnet race,
which had to be abandoned when the cook, Jo Gooding, broke her arm. She
returned to Dalkey and the phone rang two days later. It was Tracy, inviting
Angela to sail around the world in nine weeks' time. It took her about a week
to decide. After talking it over with Brendan, she decided there was no way
she could turn down the invitation. He understood the almost maniacal urge
to take on the challenge. And he would be one of the few who could see the
difference in her when she returned, such was the feeling she had of having
something so important under her belt. (Her mother, on the other hand, quite
simply did not believe that her daughter was going to embark on something so
clearly insane.)

Having decided to accept the once-in-a-lifetime offer, Angela promptly
made arrangements to leave, resigning her job of six years, getting injections
and raising finance. But she knew she was heading into the unknown. An
offshore race is one thing, but a round-the-world race is quite another. As she
says herself, 'I hadn't a clue what it was going to be like'. So it was with much
anticipation and excitement that the women of the *Maiden* set off from
Southampton down the Solent to the starting gun.

In sailing, there is a lot of work to do before the race itself starts. What looks to spectators like messing around is actually important preparation: boats tack and jib to get the best possible tactical position for the start. In the Whitbread, the opening of the race is a huge occasion, so the start is even more drawn out. For the sponsor, these boats will be out of sight of land for best part of the next two years, so a few hours in the Solent is important exposure. Pleasure craft and yachts crammed the waters, carrying relatives and friends, including Brendan and Angela's families. By the time the race started they had been out there for six hours. They were all wearing sunglasses with tears in their eyes.

Leg One: September 2 - October 7, 1989.
Southampton to Punta Del Este, Uruguay.

'You lie in your bunk in the heat, the sun pouring through the hatch as you're going to sleep. You dream you're trimming the spinnaker through the hatch with the sheet, which is wrapped around the mast, and it is perfectly trimmed. You do this for four hours, and then you are woken and told you have to get up. You can't believe it – it feels like five in the morning and you've drunk about six bottles of wine.'

And then Angela would get up and do it all over again - except this time she was awake.

The first leg across the Atlantic was full of mad dreams, the dreams of a crew at sea getting used to high temperatures and feverish sleeps. Later, they discovered that the other crews had experienced similiar dreams, but strangely the dreams disappeared after the first leg. As with many other things, the crew proved hardier on subsequent legs.

Trust was established on the first leg. The *Maiden* crew had never sailed together in a long offshore race before, and a southwestern route across the Atlantic Ocean on a sixty-foot yacht was a dramatic way for ten women to discover how they would get on.

At the time, the first leg seemed one of hard work and tremendously good humour. In fact, it was a leg of nerves. Even if they did not realise it, the women were trying to prove themselves to each other. This was also a time of learning to keep a reign on emotions, learning to button your lip and not let your temper fly. There is nowhere you can escape to on a boat. They learned to bottle up their feelings, and they rarely had huge rows.

As one of the last women to join the crew, Angela couldn't help wondering whether she would make the grade or not. Of course they all shared the same fears, but they did not realise it until later in the race. Only on the second leg did they realise how tense the first leg had been.

The first leg was also when the watches for the whole race were sorted out and bonds were formed. In an offshore sailing race, the crew is divided into two or three smaller crews, which rarely meet, but keep the boat sailing as fast as possible and on course without interruption. Angela paired up with Michelle (Mitch), her watchmate Mandy, and Dawn and Judy. She slept four hours on, four hours off, and her main duty was to trim the spinnaker and sails. Four hours is the limit on a watch like that. They tried six hours from Punta to Florida but found that they were falling asleep after a while. There is a limit to the amount of time a crew member can concentrate, especially trimming.

Angela's watchmate, Mandy, became like a sister to her. They spent every waking moment together. As captain, Tracy Edwards did not participate in a watch system, and neither did Jo Gooding, the *Maiden* cook. That left two crew members on the opposite watch whom Angela and Mandy did not get to know except in times of high drama or crisis.

As cook, Jo was an essential part of the crew. Cooking in a tiny kitchen that is pitching at an angle of forty-five degrees in stormy seas takes quite a chef to rustle up hot meals and being banished below deck during all weather conditions is not a pleasant experience. Jo was from Jersey and a beginner sailor. By the end of it, she had learnt a lot. Angela laughs as she remembers the food.

> 'It was always the same sort of consistency, like stew. The potatoes were great and then we'd have beef which was quite nice and loads of peas. For breakfast we had freeze-dried yoghurt, which was gorgeous. As a special treat Jo sometimes made fresh bread. The smell, oh you'd nearly pass out with the smell, it was so good. Sometimes she'd bring it into you in bed and she'd wake you up with it at the beginning of your watch. It was like when you were twelve, and you'd be under your blankets and your mother would wake you up, and sometimes she'd put peanut butter on it. Oh that was heaven.'

Nevertheless, the crew began to long for something crunchy to bite into. A woman's best friend, chocolate, made up for a lot of the hardship. And there wasn't much need to worry about weight either. All the activity on the boat made sure that any extra physical baggage was quickly shedded.

Angela's memories of the first leg are more about acclimatising to fellow crew members than to the weather or the uncomfortable conditions. But concentration on the task at hand demanded teamwork. This was not a jolly jaunt on the ocean but a serious race with a crew of women pushing a boat to its limits in order to get the most out of it.

After just over five weeks at sea, *Maiden* arrived at Punta Del Este to a great reception. They had proved they were part of the race — now they had to do more than just make up the numbers.

Leg Two: October 28 - December 3, 1989.
Punta Del Este to Freemantle, Australia.

'Sweat was pretty rare. If you were that warm, you were lucky.'

Mention the words 'Southern Ocean' to a sailor and she pays attention: freezing temperatures, huge seas, icebergs. All these terrors awaited the Whitbread boats as they left Punta on October 28. Angela had never experienced them. While in port, the rest of the crew did their best to scare her. Oh Angela, you've never seen icebergs have you? Angela acted blasé, but underneath she was wondering what lay ahead.

When she saw the icebergs for the first time, she was awestruck. They could have been up to two miles away from some of them, but they were still massive. Iceberg territory meant iceberg watch, one of the most dangerous and difficult assignments for the crew, particularly because of the low temperatures. Anti-frostbite and anti-hypothermia clothing were the norm in the Southern Ocean. The average weight of an individual's gear was three stone on land (and that was before the gear got wet): three pairs of socks, a pair of boots, four balaclavas (two light and two thick), a furry hat, a rubber mask, two thermal suits and a full pair of oilskins.

While on iceberg watch, the crew member was strapped onto the prow, looking ahead for the treacherous ice. With the pitching of the boat in the rough seas, the person on watch was constantly soaking and facing icy, blasting winds. Frostbite was a real danger. They were harnessed on and generally only lasted about fifteen minutes at a time. Only their eyes were uncovered, and their eyelashes were always freezing up.

Angela remembers the stress of the iceberg watch as one of the hardest things to take on the Southern Ocean. The fact that the icebergs did not show on radar made the pressure even more intense. During these arctic conditions all gear was worn, including rubber masks with tiny slits for the eyes and mouth.

It was during these harsh conditions that a problem developed with the mast, and Mandy Swan had to come to the rescue. Every day for a week she was hauled up the mast, where she worked in freezing conditions saving the rigging from separating from the mast. She was forty or fifty feet up, and every day when they brought her down she was literally black with bruising from the waves hitting her and having to hang onto the rigging with her legs. Angela had never seen her cry before, but she was crying after that.

Despite all the hardships, however, the second leg on the Southern Ocean turned out to be the bonding leg. *Maiden* found her niche in the harsh conditions. She was 150 miles in the lead and flying along. The boat was perfectly suited for downward wind conditions, and hit twenty-three knots of speed with a massive fifty-six knots of wind. The crew's bonding helped the speed as well.

In such weather it was essential that each member of the crew was harnessed on at all times. Harnesses are safety leads attached to the boat from around the body, and they are the golden rule of offshore sailing. If a crew member goes overboard in weather which is anything above calm, their chances of survival are hugely reduced without a harness. That is particularly true in the freezing conditions of the Southern Ocean, and even more so at night.

News of crew going overboard was spread from boat to boat through the evening chat shows on the radio. Five crew members went overboard during the Whitbread, and one man died. News of the death brought home a sombre realisation that what they were doing was dangerous, and any attitude short of a healthy respect for the sea was foolhardy.

One unfortunate who survived an ordeal overboard was found by his crewmates only because of a flock of albatrosses circling overhead in search of a meal. They were slashing at him like vultures. When crews heard those sort of stories going around it frightened them a little.

The 'chat shows' proved to be life-savers in many ways. A doctor on one boat saved the life of a crew member on another by instructing his mates during a crisis. On another occasion, when all the crews were having difficulty cleaning their gas pipes, Jeni Mundy discovered the simple but ingenious method of inserting a cigarette filter in the line, a tip she passed on to the other boats during a 'chat show'. *Maiden* heard the news of NCB Ireland's broken boom and of the death overboard of Tony Philips.

The last two weeks on the Punta-Freemantle leg proved to be a huge test of the *Maiden* crew's character. Tracy Edwards was plagued with self doubt, and the crew emotionally and physically exhausted. On November 28, as the boat sailed in some of the wildest weather they would ever encounter, a huge wave nearly capsized the vessel. At one point, the mast was actually in the water with the keel out of the water. Somehow they righted the vessel and kept on for Freemantle. The effort was worth it. They arrived, in first place in their class, on December 3, ahead of the men on *Rucanor*. By the time they had won the Southern Ocean leg, they had won respect from other people — and respect for themselves. They had proven to themselves that they could do it.

Leg Three: December 23, 1989, to January 8, 1990. Freemantle to Auckland, New Zealand.

Christmas Day passed by without too much fuss on the second day of the shortest leg in the race. Stockings were presented and champagne was drunk, but apart from that it was business as usual. Four hours watch on, four hours off, getting as much out of the boat as they could. Now that the *Maiden* crew were feeling confident about their exploits, the journey to New Zealand felt like a delivery – not a leg in the world's greatest race. Reality soon made itself felt however, with an injury to Tanja Visser which was stitched by Claire Russell under torchlight. On New Year's Day *Maiden* nearly lost her captain when an unharnessed Tracy Edwards slipped and was saved by Angela – or so Tracy claims. 'That happened to all of us,' says Angela modestly. 'If you saw a leg you just grabbed hold of it and that was that.'

Just as Tracy's close call did the rounds of the chat show, so too did the news that NCB Ireland's boom had broken again. As the *Maiden* crew got to

Right: *Maiden*, in the Southern Ocean, on 'lively seas'.

know their counterparts on the Irish boat better, their sympathies for them grew. The NCB crew were generally accepted to have been one of the better in the Whitbread race, and criticism particularly when it came from Ireland was keenly felt by the other crews.

'That was just horrible. The publicity hyped the whole thing up as if they were going to win the race, then they blamed the crew when things went wrong and they were one of the best crews on the race. We were very close to them and felt for them a lot. Look at it this way, I got treated so well but they got treated like shit. And the truth of it is that the boat was a load of shit. It was so unfair to the crew. Even now people heckle the guys with "JCB" or whatever. It's such a shame and it's ruined the chances of it happening in Ireland again for a long time.'

The first week in January saw *Maiden* beating along with forty knots of wind. Sailing conditions were beautiful, and the crew had the extra advantage of Mandy's local knowledge of the waters around New Zealand. By now the routine on the boat went like clockwork, and the books and tapes were doing the rounds of the crew to keep sanity intact. The lighter a yacht is, the faster it goes, therefore the crew were initially limited to one book each and only a few tapes. Personal stereos were popular for resting hours, but one of the pleasures of sailing was having a sound system on deck, where the real favourites won out. They could not bring books on deck as they'd be destroyed, so they would huddle below having a a good read – Jilly Cooper was very popular – and then they would all swap them. They had a great assortment of books and tapes. Clannad was one of Angela's tapes, and everyone loved them. She got the crew into Christy Moore as well.

Only the bare minimum of personal belongings were allowed. All sanitary and washing lotions and utensils were communal. One of the advantages of being on an all-woman boat was that they could act as they wished with no hassle. Absolutely all waste went overboard, especially after the toilets' heads blocked.

To Angela's surprise, every other woman brought a soft toy with her on the race. Angela brought a present from Brendan — a plastic globe. Brendan had given it to her for a laugh. It was a beach ball, so she hung it in the heads and put biro marks on it as they went around the world.

On January 6, New Zealand was spotted, and two days later *Maiden* arrived in Auckland to a tumultuous reception. A crowd of 14,000 was gathered on the dockside. *Maiden* had finished the leg in first position in her class again, and Tracy Edwards was awarded the ironic title of 'Yachtsman of the Year'.

Leg four: February 4 – March 6, 1990.
Auckland to Punta Del Este, Uruguay.

'That was a horrible leg.'

While the Southern Ocean had been the bonding leg the first time around, this time it was the leg they would rather not have had. *Maiden* encountered the worst of its problems on this leg though it was fortuitous that the big problems occurred when the boat was sailing through the Southern Ocean for the second time, when the women were a lot more experienced. There was now the significant element of trust, which is essential in coping with emergencies. They had already been in the Southern Ocean, and they kept asking themselves: Why do we need to do this again?

At first everything went smoothly. Avoiding passing cyclones, they crossed the international dateline without too much fuss and heard about *Rucanor* hitting a whale and the accident-prone NCB boom breaking again. But icebergs approached and squally weather brought tough times. Mikki Van Koskull was hit on the head while the boat was gybing and things seemed to be taking a turn for the worse. The atmosphere was not brilliant. They were all very concerned about the problems, and it was a matter of them pulling together to get through.

Freezing waves spilled over the deck and the bilge pumps failed. Angela and Nancy Hill worked the hand pumps and Michelle Paret injured her back. She and Tanja would have been lost overboard had they not had harnesses on.

Left: DIY dentistry — Angela goes under the needle of maiden, Claire Russell.

Angela fell onto one of the large winches and was in agony with bruised ribs. A huge wave dragged Tanja and Michelle off deck. Michelle had been on the helm and the sheer weight of the wave bent the steering wheel. Michelle's whole back arched and they thought she had damaged her spine. Claire advised her to stay in bed for the rest of the leg.

In freezing conditions, with no heat or light, the thoroughly miserable crew rounded Cape Horn. It was a very strange experience for them. They had been led to believe there would be helicopters and a big reception, but when they got there there was nothing but a lone Chilean fishing boat.

After Cape Horn all hell broke loose.

February 27 1989 will always be known to the crew of *Maiden* as 'Black Tuesday'. A leak in the boat caused chaos as the crew ripped up the floorboards below deck trying to locate the damage. All their gear had to be shifted, including twenty-seven full-size sails. Throughout, the freezing Southern Ocean was pitching and tossing the boat, which was rapidly filling with water. With the bilge pumps out of action, the leak had to be found; hand pumps could not keep the level down. By four o'clock in the afternoon of Black Tuesday, *Maiden* had taken on so much water that the level was up to the second tier of bunks below.

It took tremendous effort to get the sails up on deck. The wind was howling, and they had twenty-seven sails on board, including spinnakers. Two people were left on deck; the rest of the crew was below, trying to bail and find the leak. The boat was pitching madly, and water sloshed everywhere as they worked.

During the crisis watches were suspended, so those who were used to sleeping every four hours were up battling for twelve. After becoming used to sleeping for four hours at a time, it was like being up for three days. Then they had to take up all the floorboards. They still couldn't find the leak, so they had to switch tacks to see which was the better one for water coming in. Michelle was very ill by now, and most of the others were not feeling so good themselves.

Little did the crew of *Maiden* know it, but the other boats and the Royal Air Force were well aware of their distress. A Hercules aircraft had been scrambled on the Falklands Islands in preparation for their rescue.

The crew pulled through, however, and having given up all hope of doing well on the leg, limped into Punta Del Este on March 6.

Leg 5: March 17 - April 14, 1990.
Punta Del Este to Fort Lauderdale Florida, USA.

After the rigours of the fourth leg, the crew of the *Maiden* decided that nothing could really ever be that bad again. They were right. They had come through the worst part of the race. Now it was on to Florida and the preparation for home.

They crossed the equator, but none experienced the mad dreams of the first time round. The weather was perfect, with a lovely wind and blazing sunshine as the boat sailed on a reach all the way. The women sailed on virtual autopilot and basked like seals in the sunshine. In contrast to the bitter conditions of the previous leg, some of the crew slept on deck on the folded sails. On this leg there were many sights.

'The shrimp catchers were amazing. One night we counted forty or fifty of their boats around us — shrimp catchers with huge sets of massive lights. They looked like electric bar heaters multiplied by a thousand. They were massive fishing trawlers and they just attracted the shrimp with these lights. It was really eerie looking, and they were with us for forty or fifty miles.'

Sailing through the doldrums meant hot and very listless conditions. The crew felt lifeless. At one point both Angela and Mandy fell asleep while on watch, something which would have seemed unforgivable and impossible on another leg.

In the last week before reaching Florida, the slow, still weather changed and a fifty-knot squall kept them awake. Despite a brief appearance of leg four's mystery leak, the inclement weather did not bother them too much, and *Maiden* docked at Fort Lauderdale.

The crew caused a bit of a stir as they docked. On the completion of every other leg, the women had worn trademark pink shorts and white polo shirts when docking. By this stage all were sick of the shorts, and so in an effort to induce apoplexy in Howard (the boat's shore manager), the crew decided to don white swimsuits on arrival in Florida.

A flippant comment on the chat show forewarned Howard of the scheme; he jumped on the idea, and when the *Maiden* arrived, a media circus awaited them. What had been intended as a joke turned into one of the greatest publicity stunts of the race. The whole thing was a little odd for the crew, but the Americans loved it.

While resting in Florida for the last time, it began to dawn on all the crews that the end was imminent. Just one more leg and it was back home to jobs, family and the question of what was next.

'We were all very emotional about the fact that it was the last leg. In some ways we wished it was already over.'

Leg 6: Fort Lauderdale – The Solent, Southampton, *Maiden* set off for the last leg and home.

If the crew thought they had seen the last of the bad weather, they were wrong. The first week brought the novel experience of being caught in a tornado storm. They could see them dotted around, about five at a time. They didn't know where they were going to turn next, and they were spinning like tops without following any set pattern. Up ahead, *Rucanor* was going through the same thing.

There were also a lot of mental storms. Many of the crew did not know what they were going to do when they got home. Many people involved in sailing live very transient lives, travelling from port to port, delivering boats, getting berths on race crews.

'For a lot of the girls I know it was a case of not wanting the race to finish. There were a lot of "what am I going to do", or "what country am I going to live in" questions going through people's minds on the last leg. I was going back to Brendan, so in a way I had some of the more solid roots of any of us. That made things a lot easier for me. For a lot of the others I know it was horrible for them, though maybe when it came to the crunch they wouldn't be able to tie themselves down even if they tried. Me, I'm a bit of a homebird who likes a bit of an adventure.'

The biggest problem on the home leg was the fact that the boat was becalmed for considerable lengths of time. Just as the crew were adjusting to the notion of returning home, they had to wait for the weather and wind to decide to help them. As on every other nautical mile of the race, they were completely at the mercy of the elements.

Being becalmed was difficult as they were supposed to arrive days before they did. As they were delayed, silly things started going through Angela's head. She knew her family and Brendan were coming to meet her. Her parents and the others were sailing over from Ireland, and her mother never sailed. She started thinking that she was holding everyone up. 'But I hadn't seen them for nine months so it was absurd.'

During the final twenty-four hours before *Maiden* reached The Solent, the crew experienced a condensed version of all the emotions of the race as a whole. One of the main ones was the acute shyness. At the end of each leg they had all found it difficult to deal with the crowds, adulation and media focus. Now it would be even worse. 'Oh my God, I'll have to talk to people,' Angela thought.

The Solent beckoned, and the flotilla of boats that came to greet *Maiden* showed them what they had achieved. They had proved that an all-woman crew could sail around the world, with and against the best men in the world and beat them.

Brendan and her family waited proudly. They came out in a boat to meet her, and Angela couldn't keep her eyes off them. She waved like mad the whole way in, and then they were home.

Maiden's crew spent two weeks in a 'decompression chamber' in Southampton as they sorted themselves out.

Once back, Angela reflected on the achievement.

'I'm sure before the race there was a lot to prove, particularly among the older generation. My own friends, however, assume a woman can sail. They are never condescending. We all know that men are physically stronger than women. But if I can't winch as strongly as Brendan can, I'll get a bigger winch. But mentally I'll try and surpass him to make up. I'm probably in the position down in Dun Laoghaire now where a lot of the fellas would respect me because what I've done, so they wouldn't dream of looking down at me. But I do remember about ten years ago some would have, so I'd just get into a boat that wasn't like that. — a Boat like *Maiden*.'

Angela Farrell won a Texaco award for sailing in 1990 and the RTE Ballygowan 'Special Merit in Sport' award for the same year.

Caroline Barker
née Hutchinson

Caroline Barker (née Hutchinson) is one of the best female jockeys ever to ride in Ireland. She has ridden in amateur races for trainers such as John Mulhearn and Jim Bolger, and is one of the leading jockeys at Mulhearn's yard on the Curragh. Caroline has represented Ireland on many occasions in international women's races and has won most of those she has entered. A native of Oldtwon, just outside Newbridge, county Kildare, she and her husband Christy Barker have recently embarked on training their own mounts, borrowing stable room from Caroline's parents.

~

'Charlie Swan? Oh yeah, I beat him all right, and Adrian Maguire.'

She is a small, wiry, red-haired woman with an impish grin and a brilliant line in patter. She is matter of fact and does not stand on ceremony with anyone. In riding she is an amateur, but in attitude, she is more professional than many who would ride under the rules of the same name.

When Caroline Barker was a champion pony jockey, she beat them all. She was a teenager then, and Adrian Maguire and Charlie Swan were her regular competitors. Since then both men have become professional, and there are few who have not heard of either. Caroline Hutchinson, or Barker (her married name), on the other hand, is not known to the public at large. Yet she is one of the best woman jockeys ever to race in Ireland, and as she has embarked into the world of training, it is only a matter of time before more people know her name.

Caroline's pony championship was a national title, pursued by jockeys of both sexes. At that stage there is little gender segregation in the equine world, but as soon as amateurs make the great leap to professionalism women tend to get out of the riding game and into training. And so too has Caroline.

She now trains her own horses on her parents' farm with her husband, Christy Barker, and still rides the occasional race. She could have had a professional life in the saddle, but circumstance and opportunity mitigated against it. To be a professional jockey you need to have backing, and lots of it, and the simple truth is that it is harder for women — much harder.

Caroline may not have had sufficient financial backing or the inclination to be a jockey exclusively, but few will argue about her talent. She has the stuff that marks a special rider out from an average one — talent in abundance.

John Mulhearn, one of the leading trainers in the country, says that 'Caroline is a remarkable person in terms of her horsemanship'. Caroline works for Mulhearn in his yard and rides for him at meetings. Mulhearn is not a man who suffers fools gladly, and his employment of Caroline in his yard and as a jockey speaks yards for her ability. 'Her skill with horses is well above average and I would say that there is no horse that she cannot handle,' he says. 'I would say that there aren't many better riders in the Curragh, and that's male and female.'

Mulhearn's stables house a good many National Hunt mounts, big horses who are often difficult to handle. One such horse is 'Approach the Bench'.

'He's a big horse and a real handful,' says Mulhearn. 'He would plunge and dive around the place and when on the few occasions that he has been in America they have had awful problems handling him. Then I love to say to them, that if they could only see what a small girl can do with him in the middle of all the wide open spaces of the Curragh, that they'd be shamed,' he laughs. 'It's true too and they don't like that I can tell you,' he adds.

Small would describe Caroline. An amateur jockey carries seven pounds in weight as 'a claim' until she notches forty winners on the track. Not many amateur jockeys achieve the forty to lose their claim. In the autumn of 1994, while Caroline was getting more and more involved in her training, also she became more prominent in Mulhearn's stables. She would not, however, give up the racing until she had lost her claim. She got to thirty-nine, but the final one evaded her. So she kept riding until she got it.

'I know she is mad keen on losing her claim,' says Mulhearn, 'and she sees it as an achievement, which of course it is, but I think that it might be a disadvantage to her to do that. She is very light for the National Hunt and without the claim she'd be bouncing around a bit on the mount.'

As to whether she could have or should have become a pro jockey, Mulhearn puts up a reasonable case against it.

'She certainly had the talent to do it because she is the best woman rider in the country, but the thing is she would have to do jumps and then she would have got injured in falls. In the big jumps, it's not you that falls, it's the horse, and jockeys get badly injured. It would have been terrible to see her end up with a serious injury because that's what would've happened. There are National Hunt jockeys out there who are virtually brain dead from the amount of falls they've had.'

Caroline's ability first became apparent in an amusing way. When she was twelve years of age, a carnival set up shop at Gowran Park racecourse. One of the biggest draws was a Wild West 'bucking bronco' machine, upon which local lads were testing their prowess. When impish Caroline stepped up for a go, spectators reacted in amusement, but stayed to see if she was let on, and if so, how she would do against the mechanical beast.

The lads who were running the show decided to let the tiny redhead have a go. Up clambered Caroline, and fifty-five seconds later she hit the turf, only five seconds sooner than the winner. Sensing an increasing interest among the crowd, the lads decided to organise a playoff between the winner and Caroline –

Above: Caroline on 'Lovely Run' at Fairyhouse.

a grown man versus a feisty twelve-year-old girl. Off they went, and he bettered his time by two seconds. Caroline, not to be outdone, arranged with a friend in the audience to signal her when she had reached the target time; she was determined to win. Caroline finally landed on her rump after a minute and fourteen seconds of 'buckarooing', oblivious to the cheers of the crowd around her.

She had not noticed her friend's signal and had gone well past the man's time.

Growing up in the Hutchinson family, Caroline was bound to become a jockey and trainer. The family farm at Oldtown in Newbridge, county Kildare, was a haven for seven horse-mad children. Like most children, they had cowboy and indian battles, except that not many children can say they re-enacted the battle of the Little Big Horn with a live piebald beneath them. As children they were utterly fearless, racing home from school every evening to see who could change most quickly and get out on the ponies. There were some nights when they would be out until nine o'clock on a winter's night, clipping ponies and settling them down for the night. Of the seven children, six now live and work with horses in one way or another.

The Hutchinson children started winning trophies before they were even ten years of age. The living room today is crammed with the silverwear and cups of two decades of pony and horse racing, and Moira Hutchinson is still as proud as ever of every one of them. Caroline's first trophy is one of those in the room, won when she was all of nine, despite the fact that the opposing jockeys were all in their mid to late teens.

There was always great emphasis in the family on the showing side of the horses. Her father always believed that if a horse was not turned out as best it could be it was letting the side down. So they would spend hours trimming their manes and tending to their hooves, something none of the children ever forgot.

At that time, the family lived in Athy, where their equine prowess became legendary. They were even featured in an American television documentary called 'The Ballad of The Irish Horse'. The Hutchinson family still have a copy of the film, which is taken out from time to time, mainly as a source of amusement. On film, at the age of fifteen, is a very serious Caroline galloping on the Curragh with her father. The film progresses to show a Point-to-Point meeting, all the while accompanied by a drawling American voiceover. Caroline appears again, as serious as any jockey, in her pink silks, getting weighed in before the race.

The Hutchinsons break up laughing when they watch the film these days. The film premiered at the Shelbourne Hotel in Dublin and has been shown in the US and in Australia twice.

That was nine years ago. Today Caroline rides in many of the country's most important meetings. Perhaps the best way of exploring this woman's passion and skill is to follow her for a day at Punchestown Races, where last year she was riding for John Mulhearn. The three-day Punchestown National Hunt Festival in late April is a big occasion in the racing world, and it is a major social event.

~

Caroline is riding in a 'bumper', a race for young National Hunt horses on the flat. Her race is at 5:30pm, so there is plenty of time to savour the atmosphere of the meet. One of the first things that strikes you about Caroline and the other lady jockeys is how well dressed they are for the meet. Caroline wears a peach suit, with accompanying scarf and jewellery. True to her father's approach, she looks very well turned out.

Inside the weigh room, small groups gather and chat while jockeys queue up with saddles to be weighed. There is a smell of leather and deodorant as men with hats and binoculars peer at the large round scales. Race numbers hang on the wall like red pennants and are distributed to the jockeys. Charlie Swan and Richard Dunwoody weigh in. The riders nod hellos and say little before heading out to the paddock.

Caroline watches Richard Dunwoody win the third race for Ann-Marie O'Brien. After the fourth race, she heads inside to change. Beside the large noisy jockey's room is the ladies toilet with the sign 'Lady Riders Only'. This is the female jockeys' changing room. Inside the women are changing and a photographer is rinsing her film in the sink. The atmosphere is very chummy

Angela Farrell with (**right**) the *Maiden* in full flight.

Below: Caroline Barker on 'Brindley House'.

Above (**top**): Taking Northumberland by storm, Catherina McKiernan leads the field in the 1994 European Cross-country Championships. **Right**: In the glare of publicity after the victory. **Opposite**: Winning the Gold, 1994.

Left: Karen Nugent in her match with Martina Navratilova at the RDS in Dublin, 1993.

Left: Golden smile of victory for Sonia O'Sullivan in the European Athletics Championship Women's 3000 metres in 1994. **Right**: At the point of victory in the women's 5000 metres, 1995 World Athletics Championships. **Opposite page**: The leader of the pack. Gold medalist, Sonia shadows Szaba in the 1995 World Championships 5000 metres final.

Above: Turning on the skill.
Jeanette Turner lunges for Ireland
against Australia, Women's Hockey
World Cup, at UCD, Dublin 1994.
Below: Sandra O'Gorman,
goalkeeper of the tournament,
Women's Hockey World Cup, 1994.

Top: Angela Downey of Kilkenny after the All-Ireland Camogie Final, 1994, against Wexford. Is she wondering how many medals that is now? **Centre**: Appreciated by jubilant team-mate, B. Barnaville. **Bottom**: In full flight! Gold medalist Michelle Smith demonstrates her favourite stroke — the butterfly. And (**overleaf**) victory in the 200 metres medley at the European Championships in Vienna, 1995.

in the tiny space as other jockeys go in and out. Sandra Mullins, founder of the women's jockey association, is scheduled to be in Caroline's race, along with Joanna Lewis from England. Another woman comes in, clad in jodhpurs, and lays down on the wooden bench beside the wall for a snooze. It is Gee Armitage, who finished second in the Scottish Grand National in 1993. Caroline starts her changing ritual. Everyone has a ritual charm, something lucky to boost confidence. Caroline's is a pair of tattered orange socks.

White tights go on under the orange socks, then a white polo neck that peers from below the silks. Body protectors are compulsory to protect the jockeys in case of a fall. They look bulky but are surprisingly light. Then the white jodhpurs, made of nylon and also very light. Last come the boots, supple and brown in wafer-thin leather. All light to reduce the weight. (Though Caroline is usually about nine stone and carries weights.)

The women discuss 'pep-up' methods; things to get the blood moving, the adrenalin pumping: hot sugar with tea, Royal jelly, anything with a lot of sugar.

Caroline lifts herself up onto the bar above the shower, and does some pull-ups. Showing her strength, she zooms up and down, in her jockey gear. She hops down and rubs her breastbone and temples frantically, what she calls 'the pressure points'.

Out in the weigh room she queues up with the other jockeys, saddle over her arm. Her husband, Christy, joins her. He is equally dimunitive, and though he does not ride races anymore, he lives them through watching Caroline. While they queue she dons her red silks. 'Red for energy,' she grins. She hops on the scales — a hundred and three.

In the parade ring she talks with John Mulhearn about how they will run the race. The horse Miltonfield is being led around by the lad, just one of thirty runners. Caroline is one of three lady riders in the race. The jockeys mount. Caroline looks tiny but completely composed on top of the horse.

'She has a special knack with a horse that means she can just cut off what is going on around her no matter what, and she can concentrate solely on the horse,' says John Mulhearn. 'The animal can sense that and they relax with her completely. It's not force with a horse, no matter what its size, it's the knack.'

Christy watches the race from inside the men's changing room. A group of his peers stand beside him looking at the television up in the corner. The long room is lined by jockeys changing, with whips and helmets hanging above them.

Sandra Mullins on Gael Toi starts in the the lead, with Miltonfield in third. At 20-1 he is not expected to win, but with Caroline as the jockey anything can happen. Caroline comes up beside Gael Toi and takes over. Then Dunferne Classic moves past them both. The two women's mounts fall back. Miltonfield and Caroline finish fifth. 'She ran well,' Christy says, and the other jockeys agree.

Caroline and Sandra return, panting and sweating, to the small changing room. Caroline is pleased in spite of the result. She knows there is nothing like a race to get her fit. She can do all the riding she likes, but one race when the blood is up will get her fitter than anything.

After watching the re-run, they shower and change. Then it is time to meet Christy and head home. It is not a win for Caroline but it is regarded as a good result. The horse will have another day to prove himself.

~

At home and in Mulhearn's yard the atmosphere is different. Here is where the real muckraking work takes place. Early in the morning the horses are galloped out through the mist, their blankets flying. Christy follows the same daily routine at John Ox's stable, and in the afternoons Caroline and Christy get to start working for themselves.

The couple have set up their own training stables on Caroline's family farm, just a few miles down the road from their own home. In stark contrast to the Pilltown yard of Ann-Marie and Aidan O'Brien, the stables and barn are old, and they suit the needs of Caroline and Christy perfectly. There is land out the back where they can run out the horses, and farther down the road they have a gallops. They have twelve horses in the stables, which they work with every day. They have to cater for their every need, making sure to keep hygiene at a premium to minimise the chance of infection. All horses are sensitive, but thoroughbreds have thinner blood, and they are more susceptible to illness.

It is all a very time-consuming and expensive business, and it is impossible to survive on training alone. That is why Caroline and Christy both work for other yards. Some people may think that training horses is all about Arab sheikhs and great wealth, but the reality is very different. According to John Mulhearn, there are only about four trainers in Ireland who are making real money – Weld, Bolger, Prendergast and Ox. The O'Briens might have a hundred winners in a year, but they don't make any money out of it.

Which begs the question: why do people like Caroline and Christy put so much effort into something that is unlikely to show a return?

The profession is its own reward for the right kind of person. In their first few months of training, Caroline and Christy raced the horse Bualabus twice. They had one second and one winner, and were ecstatic with the result. The buzz of training a winner is infectious and has kept them going through the long days and hard work.

Yet John Mulhearn believes that even if Caroline makes a go of the training, she should not give up the riding as a jockey. In his opinion, she is so talented at riding that she should not leave it behind. Her talent has brought her on to the international circuit, where she has represented Ireland in Germany and Norway. In the International Series of races in 1992 and 1994, one woman jockey travelled from every equestrian nation in the world, each was given local mounts, and they raced against each other. Caroline did fairly well. In 1992 she had two winners, two seconds and a third. It was a *de facto* World Ladies Championships. Ireland does not host the event, and up to now

Above: Caroline, with 'Princess Dixieland', meets Dr Tony O'Reilly.
Below: Caroline and Christy at Laytown.

Germany has been the only country to invite an Irish participant.

There is more opportunity for women jockeys in countries like Germany, according to Caroline. Women jockeys there get many races, though the few women here would do well against the competition on the Continent. Ireland has the talent, but not the opportunities. Caroline feels that more should be done in Ireland to facilitate women jockeys – and not just the international Fidentry series. Though Dunnes Stores sponsored a series of excellent races, Caroline feels that too much money was on those races. The individual wins were worth £10,000, and the final was £20,000. It was very difficult to go down from a price like that, and the series ended up getting dropped. If the prize money had been lower, it may have been easier to attract another sponsor.

Yet even though the Dunnes Stores series is gone, Caroline believes that there are more women riding as jockeys because of it. And she points out that the Listowel and Galway meets get big crowds anyway, so why shouldn't they risk a ladies race?

So what of Caroline's future? John Mulhearn admits that he doesn't have enough horses to suit Caroline's capabilities. Jim Bolger has more, and in the summer of 1994 he used Barker's jockeying talents on a number of occasions. That Bolger employs her is more proof of her talent. The key to whether she will be a success in the training or not probably lies in whether people will give her the horses or not. What she really needs is an owner with money, time and patience, and there are not an awful lot of them around.

Caroline is a hard worker who is completely at ease working in the world of horses with Christy. She first met her husband in her teens, on the racing circuit, and they have been together ever since. Christy works in other stables and rides out their own horses but rarely rides races now. That is in no small part due to a very bad fall he had in Downpatrick in 1992. He was in front in the race when his mount fell, throwing him to the ground, and under the hooves of the following horses. His face was crushed and the injuries were so bad that Caroline did not recognise him when she visited him in hospital.

In time Christy recovered, and now his face hardly bares a trace of the damage it suffered. For Caroline herself, the nearest experience she has had to a very serious injury (apart from a broken collarbone) was riding a race when she had appendicitis. Then she rode another race only a week and a half after having the operation. What some would regard as lunacy, others take for granted.

Caroline Barker is dedicated, and little will stand in the way of her wishes and ambitions. Horses are her life, and it seems that the Irish equine world is lucky to have someone like Caroline. For the last word on the feisty twenty-six year old, it seems appropriate to turn to Chisty, perhaps the one who knows her best.

'Brains, strength, and a bit of style,' he smiles.

Catherina McKiernan

Catherina McKiernan was born 30 November 1969 in Cornafean, county Cavan. In 1989 she finished third in the national Senior Cross-country Championship, a title she was to win three years in succession from 1990. She won the national BLE 3000 title in 1989, 1992 and 1993. After four years testing international competition, McKiernan burst onto the world scene in 1992, when she finished second in the World Cross-country Championship in Boston. She repeated that second place finish in 1993 in Bilbao, Spain, and won the Grand Prix Cross-country series. That year, she also broke the Irish record for the women's 10,000 metres and reached the 10,000 metres final in Stuttgart at the World Athletics Championships. Since then, her running career has been a series of international successes: second place in the World Cross-country Championships in Budapest in 1994; winner of the Grand Prix Cross-country series for the third time running in the same year; a gold medal in the European Cross-country Championships in Northumberland, UK; and second in the World Cross-country Championships in March 1995. Catherina is coached by Joe Doonan and managed by her brother Peadar and Ray Flynn.

~

On the page of sporting history,
Let's engrave her name in gold,
To children yet unborn
Her noble deeds will be told.
Wherever athletes gather,
With pride they'll speak her name,
And say well done Catherina,
The lass from Cornafean.

These poetic words were written by Tommy Gilronan of Killeshandra, county Cavan, after Catherina McKiernan's silver-medal-winning performance at the World Cross-country Championships in Boston in 1992. As Catherina has added three more silvers and a European gold to her record of achievement since then, perhaps someone should suggest to Tommy that he work on an epic.

Catherina McKiernan's high esteem in her native Cavan is not expressed by the bard of Breifne alone. A small army of Cavan supporters now travel to the annual World Cross-country Championships to cheer on the quiet girl from Cornafean. Lawyers, politicians, showband managers and quarry owners are all part of a network that comes together in late February, when it is time to go and cheer for Catherina.

Brian Finlay, manager of Bagatelle and a former drummer with the Mighty Avons showband, compares Catherina's effect on the county to the All-Ireland football teams of 1947 and 1952.

'There is an enormous pride in Catherina in Cavan. You actually couldn't quantify what she has done for the county. There was the football team in the All-Ireland in 1947 and in 1952, there was nothing since and now we have Catherina. It's not just the sport element either, it's a lot more than that. It's pride, and Cavan is hungry for pride.'

When Catherina returned to Cornafean after her Boston success in 1992, a reception committee awaited her in Tom McSeain's bar. The pub is the focal point of no less than 127 townlands, and it lies equidistant from Ballinagh, Arva and Killeshandra. On the night of her return, twenty-four hours after winning the silver medal on a muddy and snowy course in Boston, McKiernan was serenaded by Tommy Gilronan and cheered by her local fans. Forty-five years earlier the Cavan football team had returned to their county after winning the All-Ireland final in New York, the only time the match was ever played outside Ireland. Team captain John Joe O'Reilly put a small townland on the map — Cornafean. Nearly a half a century later, the townland produced another household name when this slight female runner with tremendous strength burst onto the world scene.

Catherina enjoys and appreciates the acclaim, but she does not court it. A shy woman, she sometimes wishes that the local teams would again come to prominence and deflect some of the attention away from her. 'Sometimes I wish there was a good football team or something, it might distract a bit.'

Like any other focussed athlete, she just wants to do her best. She has tremendous determination to succeed. Her tenacity has been demonstrated admirably by her consistent success in the World Cross-country Championships — four consecutive silver medals in differing but always difficult conditions. In each year, a different athlete has taken the gold, but always in silver position has been McKiernan of Ireland.

McKiernan turned to running comparatively late in life. She had always enjoyed running and hill-walking with her father, a leading member of the local beagle hunt, but for many years camogie and basketball were her favourite sports. At the age of fourteen she won an intermediate camogie championship medal and was known as being a very strong player. After school she started running with Cornafean, competing at inter-county level. Around this time it was becoming apparent that McKiernan had talent in cross-country, so she turned to local coach Joe Doonan for guidance. Doonan is from Leitrim, a fifteen-minute journey away. A teacher by trade, his skill as a coach was well known in the area, and he agreed to help out the young girl from Cornafean. In her first season of serious training, she won the All-Ireland Schools Cross-country title.

The partnership is a good one. Both athlete and coach are reserved by nature, and Doonan's calm efficiency perfectly complements Catherina's ordered preparation for races. Though Doonan may be regarded in an international context as a small-town coach, he has proved himself well able to transfer his skills to the international arena, knowledgeably recommending warm-weather training sessions for Catherina and flying out ahead of big meetings to check out courses and alter training schedules appropriately. (It was Doonan's scouting mission to Bilbao in 1993 that provided Catherina with the essential information required for performing on the fast-running surface.)

When Catherina finished school, the question of her career arose. Like another female teenage athlete from Cobh, her exploits in running had attracted the attention of a scout from an American university, and an offer was forthcoming. It was generally held in Ireland at the time, that an athlete had to travel abroad to succeed. Many Irish stars had passed through the American college system, including Eamon Coghlan, Frank O'Meara, Marcus O'Sullivan and John Treacy. Sonia O'Sullivan went to America that very year. Catherina, however, was not even tempted. She was not prepared to leave home and knew she was far too young to leave.

So she stayed put and did a secretarial course, all the while continuing her training with Joe Doonan. By now she was a regular sight running on Cavan golf course. She worked in a solicitor's office for a year and then got a job as a telephonist with Cavan County Council in 1990. She has been employed there since and worked continuously until her leave of absence in 1994 to concentrate on athletics. Catherina considers herself lucky to have found an understanding employer. She enjoyed the work and the people there.

In 1989 Catherina settled into her home-based career and daily training pattern; it was also the year she began to be noticed. At nineteen years of age, she came third in the National Cross-country Championships, a relative unknown. By this time, Sonia O'Sullivan had competed in her third national championship and was the reigning 3000 and 1500 metre champion. So who was this thin girl from Cavan?

By virtue of her third place in the championships at Killenaule, McKiernan was selected for the national squad. Two weeks before the World Championships in Stavanger, Norway, there was a training session at the Polo Grounds in Dublin's Phoenix Park. Observers on that day remember how well McKiernan handled the fairly tough workouts of ten 300-metre runs, followed by a 150-metre dash. The runners were ordered to take the lead in turns and work hard. McKiernan, the relative novice, came through with apparent ease.

Kathryn Davis wrote in *The Irish Times* that day, 'There was an indefinable quality about her running in that session. Some unused to short recovery sessions found the work-out tough, but Catherina McKiernan, running slightly wide, floated through it untroubled.'

Two weeks later at Stavanger, however, McKiernan discovered how tough the international world of racing could be. In her debut at the World Cross-country Championships she finished in seventy-third position, a daunting introduction to the scene for the nineteen-year-old. American Lyn

Jennings won the race, and Catherina would get to know her well in the mud of Boston in 1992.

McKiernan was not put off by her placing, however. It is part of the strength of her psychological makeup that she can put bad days behind her and think positively ahead to the next race.

By this time, Joe Doonan had Catherina on a daily schedule of an hour and a half training on Cavan golf course. The County Council gave her extra time off, and she supplemented her training with nightly sessions at Cornafean GAA pitch under lights. During the summer, Doonan drove her to Tullamore to train on the track, a surface which she needed to train on as well as the grass of cross-country.

Another invaluable addition to McKiernan's back-up service has been the physiological testing unit at Trinity College Dublin. Brendan Dunne, Mary Kelly and Dr Maura O'Brien have worked closely with Catherina, monitoring her fitness and endurance levels. The unit works in conjunction with the National Coaching and Fitness Centre in Limerick, and Joe Doonan has shown himself to be extremely shrewd in choosing this option.

McKiernan visits TCD every six weeks or two months, and from the results of her tests she has learned what type of races suit her. She already knew she was not a natural sprinter and that the longer distances were her forte, but the university team was able to narrow it down even more. She learned she is not built to run the 3000 metres on track. She does have to do some speed work at that distance to run a good 10,000 metres, but in her case, the longer the better.

Pat Duffy, Director of the National Coaching and Fitness Centre, is fascinated by the results of the tests carried out on Catherina. Her tremendous endurance capacity is among the best he has ever seen. He thinks she has a highly developed mental and physical toughness which is very rare.

McKiernan and Doonan have long been advocates of the 'quality not quantity' theory of training. Running up to a hundred miles a week may make an athlete feel good about herself, but it may also burn her out in the long run and lead to injuries. Catherina and Joe have always paid close attention to the effect her training has on her body and her performance. Joe has also been very shrewd in his selection of Grand Prix events for her. She has been able to use them as training and has peaked each year at the right time.

In McKiernan's first two years at the World Cross-country Championships, she remained well out of the medals, but she was improving. Her seventy-third place was followed by a fortieth, and when she was entered for Antwerp in 1991 there was speculation that she might hit the top twenty. Sadly, she had an off-day, and finished a disappointing sixty-fifth. Afterwards it emerged that she had been suffering from a virus. Once again, McKiernan and her team kept their business to themselves, and did not make excuses.

To say she bounced back the following year is an understatement. Nine months after Antwerp the World Cross-country Challenge was in full swing, and McKiernan was setting the pace. After placing sixty-fifth in the world, she was winning and enjoying it.

December 4 in Bolbec, France, she stood on the starting line alongside many big international athletic names for the IAAF cross-country challenge race. The 1990 world championships runner-up Albertina Dias of Portugal was there, as was Annette Sergeant-Paulluy, twice world champion, and Marie-Pierre Duros, the world indoor 3000 metre champion. Catherina beat them all.

After the win, her biggest to that point in her career, Catherina returned to her native Cavan and was working at her desk by Monday afternoon. The low-key reaction is typical of McKiernan and is mirrored by her incredible ability to focus herself before a race. Mentally, she has the ability to switch off, to concentrate and, most importantly of all, to relax.

That winter the season continued in winning fashion. McKiernan won in Mol, Belgium, on December 22, and in Mallusk with a home crowd cheering her on in early January. She was beaten in Portugal in February but still lead the World Cross-country Challenge going to the World Championships in Boston in March.

Her preparations for a big race were by now impeccable. As well as the guiding light of Joe Doonan, her brother Peadar was now well involved in her athletics career and was beginning to handle sponsorship and finances. He had become her agent in all but name.

Having Boston as the venue for the 1992 championships added a few more strings to the bow of the Cavan girl. Apart from partisan support that was virtually guaranteed, the proximity of Irish athlete John Treacy was a huge bonus.

'We went out a week early to the States and stayed with John Treacy in Rhode Island. It was like a home from home situation really. He was great support and his family were all around so it was also nice and lively and distracting,' remembers McKiernan.

Treacy went out training with McKiernan and gave her all the advice he could — as former World Cross-country Champion twice over.

'He was really a tremendous help and if there was absolutely anything you wanted he would get it for you. When I was training beforehand, he came along and he brought me to the local golf course so I could continue the kind of training I had been doing. It was great to hear his views and where he thought he might have gone wrong on previous occasions.'

After a week's preparation it was up to Franklyn Park in Boston for the race itself. The presence of Treacy and her brother Peadar became all the more important since Joe had to return home suddenly due to the death of his mother. In Boston, meanwhile, a muddy Franklyn Park was made even more treacherous by a layer of snow; a tough race was in store.

Catherina had never run in snow before, but it never occurred to her that it would affect her. The day was a triumph for the Irish women's team. Sonia O'Sullivan finished in seventh place, the team finished fourth, and McKiernan, hot on the heels of winner Lyn Jennings, took the silver medal.

After the high of the silver medal, Catherina returned to training and a daunting new challenge: the 3000 metres in the heat of Barcelona. The track has never been her most comfortable surface, and the 3000 metre distance was not her ideal distance, but when a nation looks forward to dreams in the Olympics, such thoughts are banished.

Before the games began, Catherina travelled with the Irish track and field team to the south of France, where a training camp was set up for a fortnight to help the athletes acclimatise.

With Sonia O'Sullivan winning her heat, similiar efforts were expected from McKiernan by the uninfomed, but it was not meant to be. She did not qualify for the final, and it was a clearly exhausted McKiernan who faced the television cameras and press after the race.

'I was actually very happy with the way I ran in Barcelona, what with the heat and the humidity and everything. The distance didn't really suit me, I would have been far better off running a 5000 but it had to be done. I don't like making up excuses but I was actually happy enough with it at the time. The time wasn't a personal best but it was the end of the season.

'Because I was second in the World Cross-country, people thought I was going to do something better in the Olympics. I'm not trying to put people down but some people don't know any better. They think that every time you put on your spikes you are going to win a medal and it's not like that.'

Barcelona faded into memory, and with it the 3000 metres and the inevitable comparison with Sonia O'Sullivan. Barcelona was the last time the two athletes competed against each other in the same event until Paris in September 1994. The separation, accidental rather than deliberate, has probably benefited them both. They are very different individuals with hugely contrasting styles of running. Comparisons are inevitable, however, given their age, sex and nationality.

It is amazing that two such talented athletes from a small country could have been born within two days of each other. Sonia is the elder by a whopping forty-eight hours. Parallels have also been drawn with the two great male athletes Coghlan and Treacy, and it is not hard to see why. O'Sullivan and Coghlan are middle distance runners with a speedy kick and an American edge. Treacy and McKiernan have performed their greatest feats running in mud, or in the cold of winter precluding Treacy's tremendous silver medal in the marathon of the Los Angeles Olympics. The marathon could well be what Catherina will excel in.

O'Sullivan has illustrated the benefits of taking an athletics scholarship to the US, although she herself would probably express a few reservations about the system. Catherina, on the other hand, has debunked the notion that you have to travel abroad to be successful.

The winter of 1992 drew in, and Catherina was back on her favourite surface. She continued to work as the telephonist and receptionist in Cavan County courthouse, and many a visitor, voluntary or not, was temporarily distracted from their plight by the sight of the familiar-looking girl at her desk.

Catherina's lunchtime runs on the golf course continued, and such was the frequency of her appearances and the affection in which she is held by the members that she was made an honorary life member.

Having won the World Cross-country Challenge Series (worth $10,000) the year before and a world championship silver medal, the question was whether she could match such a brilliant year. It was soon answered.

McKiernan was suffering from a virus in the first IAAF cross-country race of the season, and she finished a comparatively disappointing third, but by December she was proving that her exploits of the previous year had not been a fluke. Mol in Belgium once again proved to be her victory path, and she took particular pride in demoting Kenyan rivals Esther Kiplatac and Lydia Chermoei to second and third. She opted not to run at Durham, choosing instead the January meet at Mollusk, a venue at which she had traditionally performed well. This year was no exception, and in the absence of Sonia O'Sullivan (due to injury), McKiernan took the tape in her stride. A strong run in Seville, her final preparatory race, also put her in the lead in the World Cross-country Challenge rankings.

The 1993 World Cross-country Championships were held in the Bilbao suburb of Amorbietta on March 28. A few weeks earlier, while Catherina regained her Irish national title at the BLE Championships in Dublin's Phoenix Park, Joe Doonan was conspicuous in his absence. He was once again working ahead on her behalf, having a good look at the course in Amorbietta. And what a good idea that was.

The news that the course was flat, lush and fast came as no surprise to Catherina. Doonan had returned from his trip and adjusted her training schedule accordingly to cater for a fast pace. More importantly, Catherina's mind was also adjusted. With O'Sullivan absent, the Irish focus was on Catherina, and Joe was determined to make sure they prepared as well as they could.

Joe also arranged for their party to travel ahead of the official BLE squad, which gave Catherina an extra day's preparation and acclimatisation. As it was, many of the other Irish athletes felt their arrival at midnight on Friday, for a Sunday morning championship, was too late. McKiernan was by then well settled in. She was also feeling good about herself, the logistical preparations, and her winter training in Cavan.

In Bilbao they found a local park where Catherina was able to continue with her Cavan schedule. During the winter, the weather in the Basque region of

Right: Catherina in action.

northern Spain is not unlike Ireland's unless the sun comes out. Spring flashes of sunlight raised the temperature, but there was nothing too extreme.

On Friday afternoon in Bilbao a press conference was held focussing on the favourites for the race. Lyn Jennings was in attendance, as was Elana Meyer and Zola Budd-Pieterse of South Africa. Catherina McKiernan was scheduled to appear, but an empty chair replaced her.

The presence of the two South African athletes at the conference was no accident (though Budd had not been invited). This was the first showing of a South African athletics team since the Olympics, and they were letting people know they were back in town. Their confidence oozed, and for the three days prior to the race the green and yellow tracksuits and distinctive accents were

Right: Catherina McKiernan with her silver World Cross-country medal and Grand Prix trophy, Dublin airport, 1993.

everywhere. At the conference it was acknowledged that the race would be very tough and fast, with one of the best fields ever. Meanwhile, Catherina was limbering up in the park or shopping.

She was well prepared.

'I enjoyed the build up to Bilbao. Friday I did some training and on Saturday I read a book for a while and then went out. I had been told ages beforehand that it was going to be a very fast race so I was well prepared for that. You have to try and think as positively as possible and I had run in Seville and that was really fast so that helped me. I knew then that I was able to run on any kind of surface and that gave me confidence. Then when I saw the course I was fairly relaxed and stayed positive.'

The morning of the race dawned damp and misty, just what the Irish camp wanted. The athletes were bussed to the course, and Catherina started slowly limbering up under the guidance of Joe. While she stretched in relaxed fashion she encountered a bunch of her travelling army of supporters, all slightly the worse for wear after the excesses of the night before. 'Are you thirsty lads?' asked McKiernan, laughing. Just then the reigning world champion Lyn Jennings sped by in reflector wrap-around sunglasses and white gloves. The contrast could not have been greater.

Joe observed proceedings from behind the shoulder of Brendan Foster, who was commentating from his monitor for the BBC. The race began. Budd-Pieterse made a strike for the front, and a pack followed, with Catherina in the middle. As the race wound its way around the course, Peadar McKiernan, as he now does in all her big races, ran around the inner circle following its progress and shouting encouragement to Catherina. In the third kilometre, Meyer broke and took Pieterse, McKiernan and Dias with her.

At the three-kilometre mark Meyer appeared to weaken, and the others carried on, with Pieterse leading and McKiernan in second. The South African surprisingly faded and Dias went for it, building up a gap over McKiernan. At 5000 metres Dias was away, and a visibly hurting McKiernan strained to keep up. Lyn Jennings's sunglasses glinted in the background as she made a dash for third. The media stood up to see who would get it, and the Irish supporters screamed their encouragement.

McKiernan sat smiling in the post-race press conference wrapped up in the familiar anti-chill tinfoil wrap of marathons and cross-country.

She declared herself 'very happy with my race especially as it was so fast and tough. I felt strong throughout until the last bit which is probably the first time that I've really hurt in a race. I just kept with Albertina Dias and I thought maybe I could catch her because I could hear people starting to shout at me. I was feeling some pain all right but I knew I had to today. As I said I'm really happy with the way things have gone.'

'Catherina grew up today, she really did,' said Joe Doonan. 'Today she established herself as a world class athlete.'

But she was still the shy woman of Cornafean. That night in Bilbao, as her Cavan supporters celebrated in the local hotel, boosted in numbers by the English contingent, inevitably lead by Brendan Foster, McKiernan slipped in quietly to the bar, unwilling to join in the mayhem. She smiled, accepted congratulations demurely, and refused all offers of drinks. Then she went off to bed, the slight, shy world silver medallist, with a Danielle Steele novel clasped in her hand.

That summer, at the World Athletics Championships in Stuttgart, the media and Irish public watched to see how Catherina would cope on the track in hot conditions. This time she was running in the 10,000 metres, but she was still a novice at the event. Earlier in the summer she had qualified for Stuttgart with a run that broke the Irish 10,000 metres record. She had travelled to Portugal with Joe Doonan for two weeks of warm-weather training, but would all this preparation substitute for experience?

Eighteen months earlier John Treacy had warned Catherina against running the 10,000 metres too young. In hindsight his advice was correct; it became apparent in Stuttgart that the twenty-three-year-old McKiernan still had a lot to learn about track racing. She qualified out of her heat, but was suffering badly from blisters. Team manager Fr Liam Kelleher advised her not to run in the final, but she persisted. On the day, Kelleher was proven right as McKiernan was forced to drop out before the race ended, the blisters had been too much.

Catherina's troubles were overshadowed by the Chinese middle-distance runners and Sonia O'Sullivan. After the championships, Sonia continued on her Grand Prix circuit and Catherina quietly returned to Ireland. After the problems of Stuttgart, it was time to look at what had gone wrong before embarking on another cross-country season.

Later, it became apparent that the shoes Catherina had worn in the 10,000 metres had caused much of the damage. The thin soles that she was used to wearing in cross-country races were not suitable for the hot conditions of Stuttgart. In the August heat, the temperature of the rubber track was palpable through the thin soles of the shoes. Her shoes were burning her feet and blistering them.

After a few weeks rest, Catherina returned to her training and limbered up in three local races. Bolbec in France was the first big cross-country meet of the season, and a rematch with Albertina Dias of Portugal awaited. Two days before her birthday, McKiernan came back to the course where she had launched her international athletics career, and she recorded a win in a tight race. With much satisfaction, McKiernan scraped the tape ahead of Albertina Dias to take the first scalp of the season, and she knew then that Stuttgart had not left any permanent scars.

Dias got her revenge before Christmas, but McKiernan's consistency earned her two seconds and a first by the end of the year. Mollusk in Northern Ireland, traditionally a happy hunting ground for Catherina, beckoned in January, and plenty of her supporters headed north to support her. The expected win did not materialise, however, as the young British athlete Paula Radcliffe surprised the Cornafean athlete by taking the tape. Catherina looked as if she did not have it in her to go after Radcliffe once she took off, and she commented wryly, 'Let's just say it was a very windy day'.

If Mollusk was a low point, McKiernan typically bounced back in February with victories in Seville and the Algarve. Running on sandy ground in the Portuguese sunshine was not a condition she was used to, but a burst of speed left her opponents in her wake, including the world champion Dias.

After returning to Ireland to represent her club in the national championships, McKiernan focussed on her big task in the spring of 1994 — the World Cross-country Championships in Hungary. The scene for the 1994 race was a course just outside Bucharest. The only athletes to have beaten McKiernan so far during that cross-country season were Dias, Yelena Romanova and Paula Radcliffe. But the promising young Briton was out of the race with an injured foot. Most of the betting money was quietly going on McKiernan, but all knew that in cross-country there are always upturns in races, and the Kenyans usually produce them.

True to their tradition, Kenya's Helen Chepngeno blazed the trail from the beginning, leaving the pack trailing. After the first three laps of the short but hilly course, McKiernan remained at the back of the leading group. She moved gradually through the field, pipping her competitors one by one. She explained afterwards that she was happy to remain on the rails until the congestion sorted itself out and gaps appeared. She knew it was the best place for her to be.

Chepngeno had built up a gap of about twenty metres, and despite the efforts of Zola Pieterse nobody had caught her yet. McKiernan followed immediatly when Dias went for a break, and they were joined by the other Portuguese runner, Ferreira. With the odds stacked against her, as it was obvious the gold was beyond her, McKiernan pressed on the accelerator on the last turn and left the two Portuguese in her wake. A sprint, an amazing thing to see from the Cavan woman, won her the silver and her hat-trick.

The traditional Cavan contingent of supporters let their joy be known by dancing in-between the corrals of the racecourse.

'Somebody up there was praying for me,' said McKiernan. 'With 600 metres to go, I had almost settled for fourth place and then I passed Albertina Dias, and when I got up to Conceicao Ferreira I realised that I might pass her too.'

And as for the sprint at the end, the secret was revealed. 'Those 300 metre intervals, in what was the hardest winter of training that I have ever had, finally paid off.'

Her win over Dias had also crucially won her the Grand Prix title for cross-country for the third year in a row, and the sum of £10,000.

One of the first people to congratulate Catherina McKiernan, apart from her coach Joe Doonan, was the former world 1500 metre record holder, Steve Ovett of Britain. 'You ran a great race and no one could have done better in the circumstances,' he said.

An hour after the race had ended, after Catherina had warmed down, talked to the press, and calmed herself, she spoke to Ovett again about her plans for the future and in particular, her track career.

'I'm going to do things differently. I never had the chance to recover from last year's cross-country season because I was getting ready for the track to get my qualifying time for the World Championships, but I'm in no rush for this year's 10,000 metres in Helsinki.'

A trip to Albuquerque and altitude training was the new ingredient for the 1994 track season. Closely monitored by Mary Kelly and the other doctors at Trinity College, Catherina and Joe headed off for a few weeks to the high altitude conditions of New Mexico. That she had taken special leave from her job meant that it was now possible to make the extra effort and give a hundred percent commitment to her training.

The benefits paid off when she finished second in her first track race of the season in Seville, after having had a runout in Mick Dowling's five-mile road race in Dublin. She returned to Ireland again in June and won the Europa Cup 10,000 metre race, smashing the Irish record. She finished fifth place on the track in Nice, and then the European Championships beckoned in Helsinki at the end of the summer.

The preparations seemed to be right, and McKiernan had certainly appeared to be in good form on the track, but those anticipating an Irish double along with Sonia O'Sullivan's gold in the 3000 metres were to be disappointed. Memories of Stuttgart came flooding back as McKiernan lagged alarmingly behind in the early stages of the race and then finally dropped out.

This time her failure could not be blamed on the spikes or on fatigue, as the build-up appeared to be perfect. Catherina returned to Trinity College and their reliable tests to see if they could detect anything awry. They discovered that the after-effects of altitude training were to blame. This was the first year McKiernan had tried altitude training, which is known to affect different athletes in different ways. Though the initial signs suggested that Catherina was greatly boosted by it, Dr Mary Kelly came to the conclusion that the Cavan runner had suffered a secondary detrimental effect, which only kicked in, a few months after the training, at the time of the European Championships. This seemed to be the most logical explanation. McKiernan now had to get back to full fitness and get at least one strong result on the track before the end of the season, for the sake of her confidence if nothing else.

Two weeks after Helsinki, McKiernan ran in the 5000 metres at the Berlin Grand Prix. (Ironically this was one of the Grand Prix events that Sonia O'Sullivan missed due to fatigue.) After 1200 metres, McKiernan boldly took the lead, and there she remained for some time until Britain's Alison Wyeth began to haul her in. To be in the lead with only three laps to go was the confidence booster she needed, and although she would have greatly preferred to win, a third place was just the tonic. No matter what the training, the experience of running in the showbiz atmosphere of a Grand Prix race cannot be simulated. Only experience and success at them will acclimatise a runner to the buzz of a big occasion.

Berlin having gone well, McKiernan decided to go to Paris for the Grand Prix final of 1994. She was entered in the 5000 metres and so was Sonia O'Sullivan. Ireland's two outstanding women athletes had not run against each other since Boston in 1991. This was their first track meeting since the Irish national championships back in 1989. O'Sullivan was running to win the overall Women's Award in the Grand Prix Series, and McKiernan was aiming to finish her season on a reasonably satisfactory note.

O'Sullivan was set to run a fast pace to get enough points to beat off rivals Jackie Joyner-Kersey and Svetlana Dimitrova in the battle for the overall prize. To win, the Cork woman needed to get close to her Irish record of 14:50, which meant running laps of around seventy-one seconds.

As the race began, nobody seemed willing to keep up the pace with O'Sullivan; she was on her own for the first few laps. The pace was incredible, and as she inevitably slowed, she was joined by another in the purple gear of Reebok Catherina McKiernan. Cavan faced Cork on a track in Paris with the world looking on.

With 1000 metres to go McKiernan stuck to O'Sullivan's shoulder like glue, and for a while it looked like the Cornafean woman was going to cause quite an upset. O'Sullivan, however, dug deep to stretch out ahead, and then McKiernan was caught by Borischova of Russia and Wyeth of Great Britain. McKiernan finished in fourth, proving that with the right form she could mix it with the best on the track. There was no overall win for O'Sullivan, though she received £20,000 for finishing third. For McKiernan there was immense satisfaction.

For many athletes, the end of the summer track season means a time to rest. The cross-country runner, however, is just beginning to gear up for a new autumn season at that point, and McKiernan went straight into training. This was also a special year, as the inaugural European Cross-country Championships were being held at Northumberland in Britain on December 10.

After some unusually mild weather, December arrived. Although McKiernan was used to tough conditions and difficult running, she was still taken aback by the sight of the course at Alnwick Castle in Northumbria. The course itself was only 4500 metres long, 1500 short on the originally stated length. As for the conditions, Catherina had seen better in the fields of Cavan.

Not one to let such things get her down, McKiernan prepared as usual and put the disadvantages of the course behind her. The biggest challenge came once again from Portugal in the form of European 10,000 metre champion Fernanda Ribeiro, who made her intentions clear early on by running out front, on her own. As Ribeiro blitzed the first kilometre in three minutes and fifteen seconds, McKiernan remained comfortable in fifth place, letting the gaps open up ahead as usual. She gave supporters a fright when she appeared to drop out of the race by ducking under the side tape. In fact, she was following the true line of the course and jumping over a log, as the other runners followed the TV buggy. It cost her about fifteen yards and three places, but she still looked comfortable. Because of the short distance of the course, however, she could not afford to be too relaxed.

During the second lap, Catherina moved stealthily into third place behind the Portuguese leader and the Spaniard, Vaquero. The end of the course was

Right and below: Racing for gold at the European Cross-country Championships 1994.

steep and deceptively long, as the course designer had warned the athletes. Vaquero burst past Ribeiro for the finish too soon. McKiernan went with her. She is always stronger over the second half of a race (hence her concern over the shortening of the distance), but she need not have worried. She injected a burst of speed and, fighting a head-on wind, overtook the Spaniard and finished two seconds ahead of her. Gold at last! 'There is an extra buzz to winning the gold. And maybe if I'd come second again, I wouldn't have been able to face people,' she laughs.

With four world silvers and a European gold, Catherina McKiernan has built up quite a collection. Winning the gold was special, and her determination to win the world gold was clear when she immediately started training in February 1995 at altitude for the next world championship. She went back to New Mexico having learnt the lesson of her previous training. With the help of the team at Trinity and Joe Doonan, she worked out a regimen aimed at success in the World Cross-country Championships in Durham in March.

Again, the main rivals were the Kenyans. But it would be an Ethiopian victory this time, as Derartu Tulu, the Olympic 10,000 metres champion, made a break with 1000 metres to go. Though Catherina hung with her almost to the end, she had to settle for silver yet again, despite the cheers of her supporters (among them, for the first time, her father, John).

Catherina McKiernan is a rare phenomenon. A home-grown Irish athlete who eschews the glamour and opportunities of scholarships and travel, she has worked hard at developing her considerable talents and will reap the rewards for years to come. She has four major international championship medals, with many more certainly to follow. She has not yet come anywhere near fulfilling her potential as an athlete.

McKiernan has developed as an athlete and as a woman. She has earned a considerable amount of money, but she is modest in her evaluation of it and the importance she places on it. It was only in early 1994 that she gave up full-time work, and even then she only took special leave from Cavan County Council. A house in Dublin is one of her few purchases. In January 1995 McKiernan embarked on a new clothing contract with Adidas, a wise move as Sonia O'Sullivan was already familiarly associated with Reebok. Her brother Peadar continues to act in a management capacity, but with the important addition of former Irish international athlete Ray Flynn, now an America-based agent.

While 1995 may have promised to be the year that delivered on Catherina's track potential, it was not to be despite showing phenomenal early results.

McKiernan ran a stunning time for the 10,000 metres in Lille, France in May, thus throwing down a gauntlet to her potential opponents at the World Championships in Gothenburg. She smashed her own Irish record, and ran the fastest time in the world for the distance so far that year.

However, just as everything was going so well, disaster struck.

1995 seemed to be the year that McKiernan and her coach Joe Doonan had planned everything perfectly. She had made two trips to altitude, one to Albuquerque and one to the French alps, and had not overrun after either. Races were chosen carefully in order to avoid the burnout factor.

Oslo was scheduled to be the last big run before Gothenburg. Irish television viewers watched Sonia O'Sullivan win her 5000 metres, but did not see McKiernan feature in the 10,000 as the Cavan athlete fell behind too early.

In retrospect, McKiernan should have dropped out of the race, but she kept going, probably because she had too many recent memories of unfinished track battles. If the problem had been aerobically related, or a form issue, it would not have been so bad, but as McKiernan ran on, she was exacerbating an injury to the instep of her foot; one which she had suffered from earlier in the year, but which was now back, at exactly the wrong time.

With such a short lead in to the World Athletics Championships, the writing was on the wall from the beginning, but naturally McKiernan didn't want to give up. She underwent intensive physiotherapy in London with Ger Hartmann, the man who had done so much for Sonia O'Sullivan and many Kenyan athletes. The Florida-based Limerickman was temporarily resident in London for the few weeks before Gothenburg, having been hired by Kim MacDonald. He was in effect 'tuning up' MacDonald's stable of athletes.

Hartmann did what he could with Catherina, but it seemed that the injury was stubbornly refusing to shift. With just over a week to go, Catherina still did not officially withdraw, hoping that if the heats of the 10,000 metres were dropped at Gothenburg it might give her a few precious more days' recovery time. That was irrelevent in the end, however, and the Cavan athlete was forced to admit defeat and pull out of the Irish team.

Psychologically, it was a huge blow. This was her chance to prove herself on track, just when she had been showing that she had the potential to win a medal in the 10,000 metres. Once again, she had to sit idly by. She watched on as Portugal's Fernando Ribeiro took the gold medal in the 10,000, and then Sonia O'Sullivan stood on top of the rostrum after becoming the women's 5000 metre World Champion.

The forthcoming winter brings with it the World Cross-country series once again, but it is virtually certain that Catherina McKiernan's mind will be focussed on next summer and the Atlanta Olympics. There, all going well and injuries aside, she may yet have her chance to prove herself on the track, to the world and to the Irish public watching at home; watching the biggest stage of all, the Olympic Games.

As she has matured as an athlete, she has become far more outgoing as a person. The shy woman who retired to read her Danielle Steele novel after winning the silver in Bilbao in 1992 is now far more willing to talk to fans and reporters.

And she says herself, 'I want to do really well and be really strong and fast. I enjoy the training and the preparation that goes along with it. I'll keep going though, until I get fed up and regard it as a chore.'

May that day be a long time coming.

Karen Nugent

Karen Nugent was born in 1976 in Ballyboughal, county Dublin. She started playing tennis at seven years of age and won her first first major tournament, the Donnybrook under-eleven, at age nine. The following year she represented Ireland for the first time, and she played for Ireland in the European Championships twice at under-fourteen – Bulgaria in 1989 and Moscow in 1990 – and twice at under-sixteen – Spain in 1991 and Germany in 1992. Karen has been a full member of the Irish national tennis squad since its inception four years ago under Matt Doyle. In August 1993 she won the International Tennis Federation ranking tournament in Sutton, and the Irish Open. She came second in the Irish Close Championships in Donnybrook, and she competed in both the Junior US Open and Junior Wimbledon. In October 1993 Karen was chosen as the sixth participant in the TSB Women's Tennis Classic in December, where she played world number three Martina Navratilova, losing 3-6, 2-6.

~

In December 1993, at the TSB Women's Tennis Classic, seventeen-year-old Karen Nugent relaxed with journalists who had been covering the event. She held on tightly to a pair of women's tennis shoes. Martina Navratilova's shoes. 'I'm not letting them out of my sight,' she grinned.

Like young female tennis players everywhere, Ireland's only female professional tennis player has dreamed of filling Martina's shoes. Karen Nugent may be young, with all the odds against her, but in July 1994, when she qualified for the quarter-finals of junior Wimbledon, she went further than any Irish junior tennis player ever towards emulating the achievements of her idol.

Karen has the shots, the tennis talent, and the single-minded determination to succeed in the international arena. According to Irish national tennis coach Matt Doyle, she is probably the most talented junior tennis player Ireland has ever had, male or female.

For most of the Irish public, Karen's match against Martina was the first time it had seen her and her trademarks – the bandanna, the contorted face and the clenched fist. Who was this kid at the RDS, so frozen with the occasion that she couldn't remember anything after it, but not so terrified that she wasn't afraid to ace Navratilova? They read about her again that summer. While all the madness and hype of the World Cup was going on, Karen Nugent sneaked into junior Wimbledon and defied the rankings by reaching the quarter-finals.

Karen Nugent first picked up a tennis racquet when she was seven years of age. That was 1983 in Ballyboughal, north county Dublin, and the Nugent family were playing on the front drive, a normal summer's activity for any young family.

James Nugent, however, was keen that one of or all of the children take up tennis and play the junior circuit in Ireland, just as he had done in his youth. The kitchen in the family home is graced by a black-and-white photo of the young James, a smiling curly-haired boy bedecked in whites and carrying a cumbersome wooden racquet. He enjoyed the sport so much he was eager for his children to enjoy the game and excel at it.

At first it was Mark Nugent who received most of the encouragement. James assumed at the time that his eldest child would be the one to go into the sport, not the hyperactive Karen, who ran around them while they were playing, trying to get in on the action. But the six-year-old Karen persisted, hitting a ball against the wall of the garage, picking up the stray balls around her father and brother, and hitting them back when she could.

Soon the centre court of the Nugents' imaginations, the driveway, did not suffice. Real courts had to be found.

When they moved on, James and Mark continued to play, letting the persistent Karen join in occasionally. But her perseverance prevailed, and James decided to take positive action with the children. He brought both children to a coach so that they wouldn't learn bad habits.

Only ten years later, Karen Nugent would ace Martina Navratilova to go 30-love up in the second game of the her match with the world number three.

Karen's first coach was Colette Nugent's cousin Roger Geraghty, who was attached to Malahide Tennis Club. Geraghty was not long in spotting that the seven-year-old girl had a natural talent, and he stuck with her for five years, until her cousin Michael stepped in.

In his sixteen years of coaching, Roger Geraghty had not seen a more talented female player – though at the time she was less than four feet tall. From around age eight, Karen developed a fondness for coming to the net and attacking, so her lack of height did not help matters as opponents loved to lob her. Her style marked her out from others. The world is overstocked with hopeful baseliners, and they would be welcome fodder for the young Karen, a natural serve and volleyer.

Such a player has to cover the entire net area on the tennis court, but when the attacker barely peers over the net, she has to be extra sharp in her accuracy. Back then Karen hated groundstrokes. But practising with Michael helped her develop a variety of shots. In the meantime she started entering tournaments, discovering to her glee that she was well able to win them.

She won her first tournament as an eight-year-old in an under-fourteens competition in Dundalk. She received a small cup and an even smaller amount of money, and she was now on the trail. She also played Fitzwilliam for the first time when she was eight. She didn't win the tournament, but her talent was on display and warnings of 'burnout' were heard. In fact, a type of burnout did affect her later, but it was more a crisis of apathy than anything else, something she has always had to fight against.

At nine years of age she won her first major title, the under- elevens section of Donnybrook, a class-one tournament. She also won in North Kildare and earned a number one ranking among the nation's under-twelve tennis players. Karen was not bothered by pressure at this age, but she was beginning to pick up some injuries. Her activities in other sports as well as her tennis resulted in stress fractures.

At the age of ten Karen was picked along with three others by Dr Harry Barnaville to travel to England and play in tournaments there. The doctor regularly brought Ireland's youngest and brightest tennis hopes to compete in England in the early eighties. The concept was a remarkably progessive one, particularly for a country like Ireland, where tennis was not at an advanced stage of development.

Karen Nugent, Emma Doyle, Tom Hamilton and Paul Pringle, all Leinster under-elevens, played in two tournaments. In the two weeks, Karen played in five finals and won one, beating the English under-ten number one in the final of the Mercantile and Credit Reinsurance Cheltenham Junior Tournament, a grade-one competition.

Nugent returned to Ireland, where she lost in the semifinals of the Fitzwilliam junior Open (under-twelves), the Sandycove Junior Open (under-fourteens) and the quarter-finals of the Donnybrook Junior Open (under-fourteens), beaten by the winner in all three cases.

At age eleven, Karen returned to England with three different companions: Cathriona McCarthy, Scott Barron and Stuart Doyle. This time she won both the under-twelves titles at Pit Farm in Surrey and at Bury. While on this trip, the quartet were given a guided tour of the All-England Tennis Club at Wimbledon, the tennis mecca for all in this part of the world. Karen looked around her and took in the silent green splendour of the All-England club, hoping that one day she would play there. Six years later, she played at junior Wimbledon in the shadow of centre court.

After she was a finalist in the Irish Indoor Championships at Kilternan, James Nugent decided to bring his young daughter to Florida for a series of matches. It was a risk, and an expensive one at that, but it paid off. Karen won the Sarasota under-twelves tournament and the under-fourteens at Halendale, Miami. She was a semifinalist at Lakelands before returning home and travelling to England again at Easter.

She won the under-twelves at Ipswich and was runner-up in the under-fourteens. On returning to Ireland, she had what was the first of one of her most important wins in Ireland, the Mount Pleasant senior class two championship.

Mount Pleasant was ranked as a senior tournament, but after Karen Nugent won the title at twelve, the entrance rules were changed so that only players of eighteen years of age and older were accepted. At twelve years of age, Karen won £120 and a trophy, which had to be presented privately as the tournament was sponsored by Heineken, and the image of a twelve-year-old thanking Heineken was too much for the sponsor to cope with.

By now tennis was eating into more and more of Karen's life, particularly her schooling. She did her best to catch up on work after returning to Dublin, but it seemed inevitable that a parting of the ways would have to be declared. The Nugents were investing quite a lot of money in Karen. Fees for coaching and tournament entrances alone were mounting up, but James and Colette stuck with it, figuring that Karen's talent would make it worthwhile.

But adolescence and secondary school beckoned and with them complications in Karen's life. Her family also moved to a new house in Rush, and soon Karen found her attitude towards tennis changing. She began to dread practice. Apathy set in. Her play remained at a high standard, but she had lost her enthusiasm. She went to the net less, preferring to string out a rally from the back of the court. She began to lose to players she had beaten easily when she was ten or eleven. She would win a match one day, only to lose the following day.

The problem had to do with concentration. Because of her natural ability, she had not learned to focus well enough. Her technical game carried her through at a young age, but later her opponents, whom she used to beat handily, started developing their own concentration and will to win. And as with many other skills, if a player is deficient in one area of play, extra concentration and self-belief can often carry her. Karen loves being on a show court, and thus does well in big matches, such as the Navratilova match. But she has had to learn to concentrate with consistency.

After two years at Loreto Swords, things were going badly. Karen was missing more and more school time because of her tennis, and despite her parents' support, her absences did not go down too well with the school authorities.

At fourteen, Karen changed schools to Teresians in Donnybrook, County Dublin. By now Michael Nugent had taken over from Roger Geraghty as her coach, and while the relationship worked well at first, the two strong temperaments began to clash after a while.

Karen now admits that she was spoilt back then. 'I was obnoxious. I was totally spoilt, and I had my Dad wrapped around my little finger.'

The new, more liberal regime at Teresians did not help her overcome her lack of discipline, and after a year and a half with Michael, the cousins agreed to part.

Around this time James Nugent noticed that the Spawell Leisure Centre in Templeogue was looking for a young tennis player as a candidate for a sponsorship scheme. The deal was £25,000 over five years and as much publicity for the Spawell as possible. James Nugent negotiated coaching sessions with Roger Geraghty into the deal, and Karen was taken on.

Things went well at first, but after a year or so the deal fell through because the Spawell felt that they were not getting enough publicity. Karen's youth and possibly her parents' inexperience went against them. As rally driver, Rosemary Smith says, 'If a sponsor says jump, I just say how high?' In Karen's case, a bit more leaping and display of the Spawell logo could have paid off with better dividends. But often Karen would not enter a tournament if she felt that the big names weren't there, even though to the sponsor to win a few smaller tournaments would have been worth it for the sake of publicity. After that, Karen was financed by her parents, until Tennis Ireland came along in 1993. They now pay for her training in Ireland, her coaches, the indoor facilities at Riverview and some travel abroad.

Tennis Ireland has done a huge amount for the game in Ireland, particularly for young players like Karen Nugent. In February 1990 the Irish Lawn Tennis Association formally became Tennis Ireland, under the directorship of ex-patriot Californian and former Irish Davis Cup Player Matt Doyle. As well as being responsible for coaching the national squad, Doyle aimed to develop the game at the very basic levels in Ireland, and the attraction of four major sponsors to Tennis Ireland greatly helped in its establishment: the Heinz Corporation, the Irish Permanent Building Society, Allied Irish Banks, and International Aircraft Service all put in money to pay for the thrice-weekly squad sessions which Doyle held at Riverview Fitness and Racquet Club in Donnybrook, Dublin.

It was Doyle's goal to develop young players between the ages of seven and ten, and to help them to develop all-round athletic skills. After age eleven, he concentrated on their tennis skills.

It was in the latter category that Karen's needs and Tennis Ireland's requirements met. Having already represented Ireland at international level, Nugent was inducted automatically onto the national squad at a crucial time; at thirteen she was getting bored, and testing the patience of both Michael Nugent and Roger Geraghty to their limits. She needed substantial practice indoors. In Nugent, Doyle had what he wanted — a talented junior who would make the grade if she stuck at it.

Meanwhile, school was becoming something of an issue. After taking a six-month break during her transition year, the Nugents decided that enough was enough. The Nugents discussed the matter with her headmistress at Teresians, and all agreed that carrying on was pointless. Tennis was her career now, and she was better off concentrating on that.

Giving up school and devoting all of her time to tennis clearly did Karen the world of good. The cloud of lethargy and boredom appeared to lift, and with regular practice at Riverview with Matt Doyle and the rest of the national squad, a happier, calmer Karen Nugent was now playing some good tennis. Her improvement was exemplified by a by a 7-5, 6-2 victory at Riverview on clay courts over Yvonne Doyle, a player two years her elder.

That summer, after consultation with her parents and Matt Doyle, she made the decision to turn professional. She was already playing more or less full time, and as her parents could not continue to pay the bills forever, an income source had to be tapped.

Turning pro does not automatically mean hopping on the gravy train. Travel expenses, coaching hours, clothing, accommodation and tennis gear all add up. Officially, a player like Karen should receive sponsorship for all of her equipment and clothing, but it does not always work out that way.

For example, Donnay may offer you the pick of their range of racquets, but you may be happier playing with Prince. In 1993 Karen changed to Prince just a few weeks before Junior Wimbledon, and her father had to buy five racquets at £80 each.

Karen Nugent is very lucky in that her parents have been able to support her financially in her tennis career. Tennis is a middle-class sport, particularly in Ireland, and if a player wants to progress into the pro ranks, costs escalate. In a six-month period in 1993 alone, the Nugents spent £7,000 on Karen's career.

In 1993 the Olympic Council paid for her trip to the Junior US Open. Karen is an Olympic candidate for 1996 in Atlanta, so she qualifies for flights from Delta Airlines. The other costs of the trip to Flushing Meadows were very high, however. In 1994 Karen's trip to the US was subsidised by a group of sponsors and again, her parents.

Doing the circuit of satellite tournaments is essential if Karen wants to make any impression on the senior rankings. As it is, a wild card from Matt Doyle into the Irish Open in 1992 earned Karen a third of a ranking point, which got her onto the computer rankings. Without that, she would have been completely out of the loop.

In 1993 she started playing the $10,000 tournaments, or 'tens' as they are known. Success at this level leads to points, some money, and eventual qualification for bigger tournaments. Points and money are hard to come by. On the women's circuit, progress to the last sixteen of a '10' earns the player one ranking point and $200; to the last eight, three points and $250; to the semifinals, five and a half points and $500; and to the finals, eight and a half points and $1,000. The winner receives twelve points and $1600.

Consistent success leads to qualification for other tournaments, '25s' and '50s', which in turn lead to wild cards for the big tournaments like Wimbledon. If Karen were English, she would almost certainly be given a wild card for senior Wimbledon, and such an opportunity in itself earns a player a fair bit of money and points, one point alone for turning up in the opening round, and seven for a win.

To date, her biggest payday on the satellite circuit has been in Bracknell in England in 1993, when she beat the English senior number six, Valda Lake, to make it to the quarter-finals. She also made it to the semifinals of the doubles, earning herself £400 in two days.

Junior Grand Slams do not have ranking points, but they are prestige events. Karen's 1993 appearances in Junior Wimbledon and the Junior US Open were experiences on the learning curve and helped her to do well at Junior Wimbledon in 1994.

In 1993 at Junior Wimbledon Karen was due to play Barbra Castro on the opening day of the tournament. She had been told that she would be fourth or fifth on after the starting time of noon, and she took her time with her parents in reaching Wimbledon. When she arrived at 1:30, not having eaten properly, she was told she was next on the court. She had ten minutes to practise.

Castro was ranked twenty-first in the world at junior level, but Karen went 2-0 up in the first set. After Castro drew level at 2-2, Karen went 5-3 up. She thought she was going to win the first set, then promptly lost, 7-5. But she played well and won the second set. Then at 4-1 up in the final set she choked and lost the set. She left the court in tears, with the nagging feeling that she could have, and should have, won the match.

The US Open was a better experience, but again she left with a feeling of having missed out on something. Flushing Meadow is very different from Wimbledon. The tournament is famous for its hustle and bustle, and most of all for its noise – the crowds, the players, and the planes coming in to land at La Guardia Airport.

Karen did well in the first round, beating her Russian opponent, Anastasia Pozdniakova, 6-2, 6-1. The she played the number seven seed, Italian Adrina Serra-Zanetti. Having lost the first set 6-0, Karen woke up in the second and forced it to a tie-break. She won it 7-3. Rain then stopped play after one game of the third set, and they had to switch courts because of a problem with the lights. Against this top 200 senior player, Karen lost the third set 6-4 knowing she should have beaten her.

Nugent's temper has toned down considerably over the years. There is no doubting that she is a feisty, bubbly character by nature, with an attacking game, and perhaps it is no coincidence that her favourite players were the *enfants terribles* of tennis: McEnroe, Connors and Navratilova.

It was while playing Navratilova in the RDS in 1993 that Karen forced herself to keep her lip buttoned over a line call. After acing her hero, Karen served another ace, only to hear the line judge call it out. She was just about to shout *no way*, when she decided to stay quiet. A year before, Nugent would probably have gone into a blind rage, culminating in a bout of racquet throwing or umpire interrogation. But 1993 was a maturing year for her, and though she remains an emotional player she has managed to turn that into mental strength; and mental strength can make the difference between being good and being better.

The match with Navratilova was a stepping stone in this maturing process. Just after she has lost in the second round of a 'ten' in Sheffield, her mother rang her and told her she had been selected for the TSB and was going to play

Navratilova on the Friday night. Since the tournament had been announced the previous February, it was known that an Irish player would be selected to join the five international stars to play in the exhibition tournament. Karen had been hopeful, but had not let herself think about it too much. Now it was true. 'I'm definitely going to win,' she laughed.

The year before she had been in the audience and had done her best to get near the nine-time Wimbledon champion (she denies she ever said this, it's too embarassing), and now this year she would play her. Not only that, as a player in the TSB Classic, Karen was entitled to stay with the other players in the Penthouse in Jurys, and have her own car and driver for the weekend. Cinderella had come to the ball.

'Oh sure, she'll be treated like this big celebrity for the weekend and then it'll be back to life, she'll have to watch that,' said Matt Doyle beforehand. 'When you are used to playing in the qualifiers of satellites you shouldn't get used to the Cinderella lifestyle — you have to come back down again.'

Before the match, Navratilova warmed up on the RDS court with Mary Jo Fernandez. The arena was virtually empty except for workmen putting the finishing touches to the heating and lights. Karen walked onto the court. she looked shy and awkward, as if she would get sick at any moment. Navratilova made it her business to come over and shake her hand, smiling at the girl in the Ellesse track suit. Fernandez stopped and offered Nugent her end of the court. Karen walked on self-consciously and started to hit with the world number three. You could see the concentration in her face: just get the ball over the net and keep thumping it, don't make a fool of yourself. The warm-up did her a lot of good for the match later on. At least she had hit with the woman at this stage if only for fifteen minutes.

'When they said "ladies and gentlemen, please give a warm welcome to Martina Navratilova and Karen Nugent", I thought I'd die,' says her mother Colette Nugent who was sitting in the audience watching her daughter and silently praying for her. 'Once she relaxed and started playing, I was happy for her,' she adds.

Karen lost the first game, but not until after bringing it to deuce. She now had a bit of confidence. When she won her serve, she clenched her fist at her side. At 1-4 down in the first set she served a love game, and the crowd responded with an appreciative stamping of the feet. Was Martina taking the foot off the throttle? Probably, but nobody really cared. Karen was playing some good attacking tennis. Despite a weak second serve and some weak groundstrokes, she went to the net successfully and was not afraid to pass Navratilova, earning little gestures of applause from her opponent. Another serve game to Karen and a 6-3 first set seemed quite respectable. Nugent won two games in the second set, again on serve, but played some better tennis, leaving an Irish audience well impressed with what they had seen from the diminutive Ballyboughal girl.

Afterwards the press gathered for words of wisdom from the world number three about the world number 673.

'I was wondering what would happen if I lost the match to Karen,' she laughed. 'She made me play because she played very well, and I could have been threatened if I didn't perform. She played a lot better than her ranking, and if she continues to play like that she could easily be in the top 100 of the game, and that's despite the weaknesses in her ground strokes and second serve. A good player will attack her second serve and attack it very well. However, she's got a good game, a good feel for the ball and good ability. There's definitely no question about it, she could make top 100 all right. She's good at the net, she closes very well and she has all the right shots. I'm sure she's a very good doubles player too, absolutely. There's not that many players who can attack the net and she's natural at it. At seventeen I didn't have a backhand or a coach. At seventeen she probably would have beaten me,' she said modestly.

For the rest of the weekend, Navratilova took the time to hit with Nugent on the RDS court, and as the audience entered the arena before the final on Sunday they were amazed to see the Dubliner practising volleying with Navratilova. Martina helped her with her forehand volley, getting her to hold the racquet more to the side.

One member of the audience staring in open-mouthed astonishment was Clare Curren of Belfast, Karen's hitting partner on the Irish national squad. Clare stood there at the side of the court gaping in amazement with a Wimbledon souvenir bag over her shoulder. The bag was about as near as she had come to the world number three before, and now here was Karen coolly hitting with her.

According to Matt Doyle, Karen basically plays Martina's game without her strength. But he acknowledges that it takes about five years to produce a good player. Karen has been coming through for four years now, and Doyle is hopeful that she is close to breaking through internationally.

Karen's last year as a junior was 1994. She was well aware of everyone's expectations, and for a good deal of the year her progress was slow. Then came Wimbledon.

Karen only managed to participate in the tournament by default. The young Dubliner arrived at the All-England club to find that she was on the waiting list for admission to the event. Luckily, another player's no-show allowed her an entry, and she jumped at the chance.

Nugent promptly made a mockery of the seedings in the tournament by winning her first two matches to qualify for the third round. She then came up against the fourth seed for the event, Australian Anabel Elwood, against whom she employed her serve and volley to good effect. Karen won the first set 6-3 and looked to be comfortable in the second, but a lapse of concentration let her opponent back in, and the Australian took the second 6-2. In the final set the unseeded Dubliner shook herself awake and held serve to level at 3-3. Ellwood

Above: Game, set and match, Ms Navratilova, TSB Women's Tennis Classic, RDS, 1993
Below: Karen Nugent.

served, and Nugent broke to go 4-3 ahead. From there she held twice to take the match 6-3, 2-6, 6-4.

The number five seed, Korean Mi-Ra Leon, awaited Karen in the quarter-finals and another chance to play on a show court. Her opponent outfoxed her completely in the first set, pinning her on the baseline and allowing the Dubliner to win only one game. Nugent rallied valiantly in the second to win by the same margin, and it was all down to the third set. Leon got two crucial breaks and held serve to go 4-1 up. Despite things looking so bad, Nugent returned the compliment and broke back in the sixth game, but she then lost her serve and the match through frustrating errors. The Dubliner shrieked with anguish as she lost match point. It was a match that she could have and should have won, and she knew it.

While Karen may have been disappointed with the way she lost at junior Wimbledon, she had achieved her ambition for 1994, in reaching the quarter-finals of a junior Grandslam tournament. Also, she had made plenty of people sit up and take notice of her. The British press wondered how a relatively unfinanced and unseeded Irish girl could have performed so much better than their own junior tennis players. Millions of pounds had been pumped into British tennis in the previous decade in an effort to find a champion. The annual profits of the Wimbledon Lawn Tennis Championships are channelled into the British Tennis Association and their national development programme. However, despite this investment, the last time a Briton won senior Wimbledon was in 1977, when Virginia Wade won the women's title, and the furthest that any player has progressed since then was the quarter-finals. Great hope had been placed in the up-and-coming juniors, but their performances in 1994 were dwarfed by that of an eighteen-year-old Irish girl who only scraped her way into the tournament.

A month later, there was some consolation for Karen when she and her partner Kate Warne-Holland won the doubles title at the Oil of Ulay Irish Ladies Open Tennis Championships. There was not much money in the win, and it did not do a lot for her world senior ranking, but it proved for the second time that summer that if she concentrates and plays her best, she can do things. It was also Karen Nugent's first senior ranking tennis title.

It is perhaps ironic that Irish tennis found itself at something of a crisis in 1994 when Matt Doyle's contract as Director of Tennis Ireland was not renewed. Doyle had masterminded the financial injection into the sport by local sponsors, and it seemed that just as the base of tennis was developing nicely, the ground was cut from under him. Doyle was not happy when his contract was not renewed and pointed to Karen's Wimbledon achievement as part of his legacy.

Karen has now left the junior rankings, and the gulf beween the junior and senior rankings is enormous. Karen may have got into the last eight of the most prestigious tournament in the world, but as a senior she must go back to the

Right: TSB Women's Tennis Classic, RDS, Dublin, 1993.

Right: Karen Nugent with Virginia Wade at Wimbledon 1994.

drawing board and a ranking in the six hundreds. Her future successes will probably be in doubles, and if she can locate a strong partner her name could well feature highly in global Grand Slam events. That depends on her determination, dedication, and of course a healthy dose of luck.

In 1995, the harsh reality of how an injury can interrupt a promising career came home to Karen Nugent.

For the first few months of the year she was dogged by a back injury which prohibited her from playing many of the important 'ten' and 'twenty' tournaments. By missing out on many of these, she not only missed out on badly needed wages, but more importantly the vital points needed to access her to wild cards for the big tournaments. For example, because of her lack of match play, coupled with the fact that she is not English, she held out little hope of gaining a wild card to the qualifiers of Wimbledon, even if she had reached the quarter-finals of the junior tournament the year before. She had some hope for the doubles, but that diminished in the days preceding the tournament, and then it was off to the boat club in Belfast for another domestic tournament.

In terms of personal satisfaction, she could be happy in that she probably produced her best performance yet for her country in the Federation Cup that summer. Playing on clay and in searing temparatures in Kenya, Nugent and her teammates pulled off a string of remarkable victories, despite in-team illness and heat exhaustion, only to fail at the last hurdle to gain promotion out of their zone of the cup. The sad fact is that it was probably the closest that Ireland had got to reaching the upper echelons of womens' international tennis, and the chance is unlikely to present itself for a very very long time.

Following on that disappointment, Nugent had a doubles win in the Oil of Ulay Irish Open and she continued to practise at her cousin's tennis academy in north county Dublin.

Since her much publicised meeting with Martina Navratilova in Dublin, their paths have since crossed once at the US Open. 'I was walking down a corridor and she was coming towards me to go on court; she kind of looked at me like she knew me, but I was too embarassed to say hello, so there you are.'

At least she has those shoes. All she has to do is keep up with the footprints.

Rosemary Smith

Born on 7 August 1937, Rosemary Smith was taught to drive at age eleven by her father and drove in her first rally at nineteen. She worked as a driver with the Rootes Group from 1962 to 1967. Her list of ladies' prizes is impressive: London – Sydney, Monte Carlo, Circuit of Ireland (five times), Scottish International (six times), Shell 4000 (twice), Canadian Rally (twice), Geneva, Tour de France, Alpine, RAC rally of Great Britain, London – Mexico, Rally of South Africa, Safari Rally, the Acropolis and East African. She is one of only five women ever to have won an international motor rally outright. In 1965 she received the Texaco Motorsport Award, and she was voted Woman of the Year in London in 1970. In 1992 she received the Trusthouse Forte Legend in Sport Award.

~

Ireland in the 1970s was a country in adolescence. A nation that had grown up in the mothball-like atmosphere of the fifties and blinked its way through the lively sixties emerged in the seventies ready to get up and go.

In many ways Rosemary Smith was an embodiment of the spirit of the decade. She was young and good-looking, a woman in a man's world who was unafraid to take men on. But she still had to battle a level of sexism and discrimination that we would find laughable today. In a decade when women civil servants still had to give up jobs when they married, Rosemary Smith was for many women a role model and a torch carrier.

When my day is up it's up, and that's it, Rosemary has said. Unless I get to the stage where I'm being completely stupid about things, and I'll know before anybody else does if that happens.

That day, however, looks like it is still a long way away. Rosemary Smith, Ireland's best-known woman driver, is still behind the wheel. These days, crowds at Mondello Park and the Classic Rallies thrill to her hair-raising speed and courage, and the commitment and dedication are as strong now as when she participated in her first Monte Carlo rally, or when she lost the use of her gearbox and reversed her way up the Khyber Pass. 'I have a crick in my neck to this day.'

When John Smith taught the eleven-year-old Rosie how to drive in a field in Tallaght in Dublin, he could not have realised what a talent he was unleashing on the world. Rosemary herself did not realise it either, and for many years driving was simply a bit of fun with her Dad and brothers. Mr Smith was in the motor trade, and there was always some banger around for Rosemary to drive. The family had some land out in Old Bawn in Tallaght, and back then it was all fields — perfect for them to tear around in.

At school, however, she was totally distracted, so she left Loreto to enroll in the Grafton Academy to study what in those days was called dress design. Like most other things in her life, she dived in, completing her first full-time year and being voted 'most promising pupil'; but disregarding the privileges such a title might bring, she left to join a Dublin design house. She spent two years there, and meanwhile got her driving license as soon as she turned seventeen.

She was happy and skilled at designing, but even though she opened her own business on Dublin's South Anne Street, catering for the well-heeled woman of her day, she still felt she had not found the right career path. Fate intervened in the form of Delphine Biggar, a customer who owned The Coffee Inn across the street from Rosemary's studio. Delphine regularly requested the most unusual outfits: silk shirts, all-in-one jumpsuits, and lots of clothes with personalised motifs. As Rosemary bought up Hermes scarves in Brown Thomas, sacrificing them for the sake of the custom-made silk shirts, the mystery revealed itself — Delphine was rally driving.

As she was no stranger to a car, Rosemary expressed curiosity, and Delphine invited her to the next outing by announcing that Rosemary would navigate. Navigation, however, did not turn out to be Rosemary's strong point. By the time the rally was about three miles up the road, they realised they were lost. Delphine started to swear. The daughter of a Methodist, Rosemary had not heard the like of it, and listened to to her co-driver's cursing until Delphine told her to take over the wheel. Rosemary got behind the wheel and never looked back. They finished third in their class, and Rosemary was on the road.

Rosemary and Delphine drove together for some time, with the young designer eagerly eating up the miles. Her father encouraged her in the pursuit of something he also loved, and soon the pair were doing all-night rallies. It was on such a race that Rosemary had her first real dice with danger — something easy to be blasé about but never far away in motor racing.

During a rally in Carlow, they approached what they believed to be a crossroads and went straight through. It was in fact a T-junction, and the Mini slammed into a wall. The impact was so great that the roof was torn off the vehicle and the engine ended up between the drivers. Rosemary was conscious and called out to to her co-driver. Delphine was bent forwards, groaning, and as Rosemary shone the torch on her she saw to her horror that the woman's head had been literally scalped by the roof, and the crown of skin and hair was flapped back. Frightened, but cool, Rosemary replaced the flap of skin and pressed tissues on top of it. By now the blood was pouring out, so she strapped the head to stem the flow.

Leaving an unconscious Delphine, Rosemary set off in stockinged feet ('the first things you lose in a car accident are your shoes') to find help. A pig farmer came to the rescue, and Delphine was brought to hospital where the receiving medics presumed they were accepting a no-hoper. They were wrong. Delphine survived, not only to tell the tale of losing her head, but to rally again with

Rosemary within the year and complete the Circuit of Ireland.

Such an accident would have put anyone off driving, and Rosemary was no exception. That night, however, after getting stitches in her face without an anaesthetic, she greeted Delphine's husband, Frank. To her horror he ordered her into the car to drive to the hospital in Carlow. Rosemary credits Frank with getting her back on the road. 'If it wasn't for him, I don't think I would or could have driven again. He sat calmly beside me and I didn't panic once the whole way. I'll never forget him for that!'

Rosemary has had plenty of other near-misses and disasters since then, but her first brush with mortality has remained the clearest. She always keeps in mind that, though a sport, rally driving is a very dangerous one, and approaching it with anything less than total commitment and concentration is foolhardy. 'I had to work very hard at it simply because it's too dangerous. If you're flying around up on the edges of cliffs in the Italian Alps and you don't take it seriously — you don't come back. It's as simple as that.'

To sit alongside Rosemary Smith as she drives around Mondello Park is to appreciate this in only the smallest way. There are no cliffs or rock faces such as she has faced at other times in her career, but the passenger is glued to her seat by g-forces as she steers the car around the bends, all the while gently explaining what she is doing.

The glamorous woman who arrives at Mondello is slightly incongruous with the jumpsuited and helmeted driver who skims through gears at a glance. Appearance has always been important to Rosemary, and she believes that in some ways her efforts to maintain a certain look has given her a psychological advantage over her male competitors. When she started out, she was at pains not to look worn out after a race, with spanners in her pocket and streaks of oil in her hair. 'It was a case of being told, "Oh, you only got your drive because you're a bird with blonde hair or because you're tall".'

Rosemary has always chosen to silence such attitudes with achievements, though she will admit that in certain circumstances the female angle has inadvertently worked to her advantage. After her first Monte Carlo rally, she was approached by Norman Garrod of the Rootes driving group, who coolly informed her that she was going to drive for the group.

At the time she thought the invitation came because she was a good driver, but later she learned that Garrod's approach had as much to do with publicity as with her ability.

Soon, however, Rootes realised they had a very good driver indeed, and all previous motives were forgotten. The publicity angle continued, but Rosemary has always believed that if the sponsor or the company is paying you to drive for them, then you can only thank them by doing your best in the races and being available for all promotional work. As she has said many times, it is a business as well as a sport.

Something of a fluke had led her to Monte Carlo and the Rootes group.

Because of all the time that she and Delphine were spending rallying, her design business was beginning to suffer, and she had decided to give up the sport. After completing the RAC Rally of Great Britain and finishing third in the women's class, both Delphine and Rosemary felt that they had achieved about as much as they could within their limits. Then out of the blue came a telegram.

Saw you on RAC rally. Want you to do Monte Carlo rally. It was signed Sally-Ann Cooper, daughter and heiress to the Cooper's fly spray empire.

Rosemary's father knew what a golden opportunity this was, and once again his influence was vital. He insisted that she go to see this woman and take the chance. After a cool reception from the aloof and very rich Ms Cooper, Rosemary set off with her new partner and another driver for the South of France. It was an enormous adventure for a young woman in the late sixties.

The trio made it to Monte Carlo in Sally-Ann's Sunbeam Rapier, and they finished fourth in their class. Sally-Ann treated the entire journey as something of a jaunt and spent most of the journey lolling in the back seat feasting from a picnic hamper while the other two did the driving – at least until nearing a control, when Sally-Ann would take over.

When the Rootes group came calling and Rosemary accepted, not everyone in the Rootes camp made her feel welcome. She remembers an occasion near the beginning of her time in the group when one of the male drivers announced at a team meeting that he thought the men's and women's teams should share their winnings separately, when usually prize money was pooled. According to Rosemary, he thought the women would not be pulling their own and so cutting in on the men's winnings.

That year, however, Rosemary and her co-driver entered the Circuit of Ireland, the Tour of Scotland, the Acropolis, the Tour de France, the RAC and the Coupe des Alpes. They won their class in each rally. The men had a bad year, and at the end-of-year meeting the same man who had wanted separate prize pools now suggested that all the money be pooled together. Norman Garrod reminded him of his previous statement and refused.

Rosemary was driving at that time with Rosemary Seers, a technically accomplished racer who was expert at timing and the controls. Though Rosemary did not feel particularly comfortable with Seers as her co-driver, they combined for a number of years and had many successes.

One of those dangerous reminders of mortality happened with Seers – though it was also another example of Rosemary Smith's tenacity to carry on no matter what the odds. During a Monte Carlo rally Seers suffered an attack of Bells Palsy, and her right side was nearly paralysed. Smith took over the wheel, and they found themselves in second place behind the Finnish leader Tino Makinnen, negotiating the Alps in heavy snow. Driving through the night is always tough, but between three and four in the morning the body is at its lowest ebb. A moment's lack of concentration can result in disaster. Conditions on this night were about as bad as they get. With visibility at a minimum, Smith was using Makinnen's taillights as a guide. Unbeknownst to Smith, Makinnen went round an S-bend; she followed directly behind his lights and found the car sailing straight through thin air. They had missed the bend completely.

The car travelled for what seemed like an eternity and landed far below. When Rosemary called out to her partner, she saw the passenger door flapping open and Seers gone.

The car had in fact landed in a tree and was dangling above the slope below. Smith climbed out and started climbing up to where she could see the headlights passing above. Eventually she made it and frantically waved down a car. Three Germans in a Mercedes came to the rescue, and they headed down the mountain to look for the lost co-driver. An hour later they returned with a limp Rosemary Seers. All climbed into the Mercedes and they stopped at a hamlet where an ambulance was called to look after Seers. She had cracked her skull and eventually ended up in the American Hospital in Paris.

'The ambulance took her away and I turned to the Germans and I said "what about Rosemary?" "What about her," he said and we headed off down to Monte Carlo. It was then that I thought to myself, that I must really be quite tough when it comes to driving. I think maybe if I really was a dumb blonde I would have been out on my ear long before.'

Seers never quite recovered properly from that accident, although she did well to survive.

'I have to say poor Rosemary was a most unhappy girl, but me driving off the edge of a cliff certainly didn't help her,' reflects Smith.

Seers was one of many co-drivers through Smith's career, but apart from Delphine Biggar, two others stand out: Alice Watts and the woman who drives with Rosemary today, Pauline Gullick. Watts was an efficient Scots schoolteacher who loved to go rallying. She and Rosemary drove for a number of years before she ran off with a man who banned her from contacting Rosemary or rallying again. While Rosemary and Alice were in tandem, however, they met a young woman who ran over to their car and announced in a West Country accent that she wanted to be Rosemary's co-driver. At the next control and again at the end she asked again. Rosemary asked her if she could drive. The answer was no. The same reply came to Rosemary's question about her navigating skills. So, giving her an address in Ireland, Rosemary told the young Pauline Gullick to go off and learn both and then come back to her. Gullick took her at her word, and a year later a licensed Pauline rang and said timidly that she was going to be in Ireland for Christmas. Could she visit?

For five days Pauline was at Rosemary's, saying hardly a word in the chaotic Christmas atmosphere. Then she went off again to take her international license exams, all the while letting Rosemary know how she was getting on. The following June, love whisked Alice away, and Rosemary was without a co-driver for the Circuit of Ireland. Pauline called again and was immediately invited to join the team.

Rosemary knew the minute Pauline sat in the car and started preparing for the race that she was going to be outstanding. Twenty years later Pauline is still driving with Rosemary Smith, travelling from Bristol to join her on whatever the latest adventure happens to be.

Over the years they have faced many problems together. Driving through Donegal once, the throttle snapped, and Pauline had to lean into the engine and keep her finger on the throttle. Rosemary steered by sticking her head out the window, but when they suddenly hit a bump Pauline sailed through the air, landing unconscious at the side of the road.

As well as shattering a kneecap and nearly losing her thumb, Pauline later developed back problems that effectively paralysed her for eighteen months.

It may sound as if all of Rosemary's co-drivers were nearly killed, but the accidents are a true measure of the danger of the sport. But this accident came at a particularly bad time. Rosemary's marriage had broken up, and now her co-driver could barely move. She felt that enough was enough. She was the British rally champion. She had competed in all the big American races, including Daytona. She decided it was time to stop.

Though Pauline recovered and returned to the sport within two years, it took Rosemary eleven years to return to her first love – driving. The very public break-up of her marriage took its toll, and she embarked on a succession of ventures – public relations, television, even setting up a modelling agency – but none caught her imagination or proved to be a worthy substitute.

Though Rosemary now says she has no regrets about her marriage and divorce, it is clear from what she says that the support of a partner would have been welcome.

'My ex-husband liked the notoriety and he liked the money, but he didn't like the fact that he was known as "Mr Smith". He wasn't big enough to take it and he was always chipping at me because of that. If I had a man who would have backed me the whole way through it might have been different. Or else if I had never have married at all, which is perhaps what I should have done.

If I had a man who really backed me we could have had a great time together. I could also have made a fortune. I was always putting off things because he didn't like it. Like I was offered this TV show in the US and when I said it to him, my ex said that if I went to do it I needn't bother coming back at all.

'When I was young it was difficult, I wasn't married and if you are single and you have a woman friend like say Delphine, well you get talk — "Oh you know why she doesn't have a boyfriend". Then when I got married all my pals were men on the circuit and the women were threatened by me. You just couldn't win. To this day, mind you, I get that, who was she with or whatever.'

A regret which crops up in conversation is that of children. Rosemary never

Above: 'Flower Power' — Rosemary Smith in action. **Below**: Still racing after all these years.

had children and clearly for all her achievements she would have loved this. 'I had five miscarriages in all, and again rather than supporting me, my ex saw this as a way of getting at me, telling me I wasn't even woman enough to have a child.'

Despite what was obviously a difficult atmosphere to live in, Rosemary did not give up on her marriage. She did not leave and she was not the one to finally call it a day. This she sees as another example of her tenacity and her dedication to seeing something through to the end.

'I suppose when it came to my marriage I had made a commitment. To this day, I'm a very peculiar person in that if I do say something I'll do it and that is that. It was the same with my marriage, till death do us part and all that. In the end he was the one who walked out, not me. No way.'

Rosemary received news of her divorce from her husband and his subsequent remarriage through the post.

Why did Rosemary return to the sport of rallying after eleven years? Why did she choose to face the long hours, the arduous journeys and the danger? Why didn't she sit back and relax?

Rosemary loved the sport too much. It was in her blood, the only thing that she really felt happy at. Once she decided to come back, she saw at once what she had been missing. In 1965, Rosemary had won the Dutch Tulip Rally outright, defeating her teammate Tiny Lewis and writing herself into the history books as one of only five women ever to win an international rally outright. She returned to Holland and the Tulip Classic Rally in 1993. Twenty-eight years on and she was still going strong. In honour of her comeback, the rally organisers presented her with a commemorative trophy, one of the most treasured of her enormous collection.

She has come a long way from Delphine Biggar's silk shirts and starting out as a failed navigator. To this day she says her father was her greatest influence. He taught her to drive at eleven, and from the word go he was the one who told her to give it a go and do her best. If you're not good enough, Mr Smith would say, it's just not meant to be.

And that cannot be said of Rosemary Smith.

Sonia O'Sullivan

Sonia Sullivan was born on November 28, 1969, in Cobh, county Cork. She made her mark first in 1987, when she won the national schoolgirls Junior and Senior Cross-country Championships. She also broke national junior records for the 800 metres and 3000 metres and started a sports scholarship at Villanova University in the US. In 1991 she broke the indoor world track record for the 5000 metres, won a gold medal in the 1500 metres at the World Student Games in Sheffield, and broke the Irish record for the 1500 metres at Monte Carlo. In 1992 she placed seventh at the World Cross-country Championships at Boston (Catherina McKiernan came second) and broke the Irish 3000 metres record by twelve seconds. Other highlights included her fourth-place finish in the 3000 metres final at the World Athletics Championships in Stuttgart and her silver medal in the 1500 metres. She broke the Irish and European records for the women's 3000 metres at Crystal Palace in July 1994; she won gold in August 1994 in the 3000 metres at the European Athletics Championships in Helsinki; and August 1995 saw the culmination of her career to date as she became the women's 5000 metres World Champion at Gothenburg.

~

'I want that gold medal more than anything else.'

So said Sonia O'Sullivan in Helsinki on August 9, 1994, as she anticipated her 3000 metres final in the European Championships. Sonia's comment to the press was not bravado. It was the declaration of an athlete who had matured over two years of constant international competition and learned from the experience of twice finishing in the thankless position of fourth.

Eamon Coghlan has said that 'fourth is the loneliest place in the world'. He and Sonia know the disappointment of being so near and yet so far, and the fear of becoming an also-ran. Coghlan was speaking on RTE after Sonia O'Sullivan finished fourth in the 3000 metres final of the 1993 World Athletics Championships in Stuttgart. A blur of three white Chinese singlets had dashed away with 700 metres to go, and with that run they also dashed Sonia O'Sullivan's hopes of becoming Ireland's first ever female track gold medal winner, for that day at least.

She also finished fourth in Barcelona in 1992, but the disappointment then was different. A medal was a hope then rather than an expectation. The aim then was to reach the final of the 3000 metres. Sonia was still on a learning curve. She may have lost a medal opportunity, but she was still learning.

In Stuttgart the expectations were higher, and the last place she wanted to be was in the lead heading into the final bend, not knowing how near anyone

Above: Sonia O'Sullivan on her way to fourth place in the 3000 metres at the World Athletic Championships in Stuttgart, 1993.

was. Until they passed her, that is. The agony of fourth place hit home when she was asked to stay behind after the race and do a drug test. 'I just thought "Oh no. If I had finished in the top three, I wouldn't have cared, but to finish fourth ... Oh no".'

She was the favourite to take the gold medal in Stuttgart. She had blazed a trail immediately after Barcelona, smashing five Irish records in ten days and running up a succession of victories. She had purged the demons, beating the Olympic champion, Romanova, the silver medalist Dorovskiyh, and the holder of the bronze, Angela Chalmers.

The summer of 1993, after recovering from an injury which kept her out of the World Cross-country Championships, she attacked the Grand Prix trail again. Her victories included a stunning performance at the Bislett Games in Oslo, when she clocked 8:28.74, the seventh-fastest time ever for the 3000 metres and a massive five seconds off the fastest time for that year. Experts and pundits installed O'Sullivan as the race favourite for the World 3000 metres Crown, despite news of fast times coming from little-known athletes in China.

'I think going to Stuttgart I had seen the times they had got so far that year and I think I didn't really believe it,' she said when she returned to Cork at the end of the season. 'I think maybe I thought there was something wrong with their times or that something just wasn't right. I didn't want to believe they were brilliant.'

When Yunxia Qu, Lin Li Xiang and Li Lung Xiang sped off with 700 metres to go in the 3000 metres final, O'Sullivan hesitated crucially and lost the initiative. She passed Scotland's Yvonne Murray, but she was never going to get there. The Chinese triumvirate took the medals, and everyone else, by surprise. Sonia was fourth. Again.

After the race, Sonia stood at the side of the track, tears streaming down her face. By the time the RTE link-up came through she had composed herself enough to appear relaxed and smiling as she spoke to George Hamilton, but the tracks of her tears smudged her shining cheeks.

Sonia met up with her parents, who had watched the race from the grandstand. Though upset, they knew that the best they could do for her was to be supportive. John and Mary O'Sullivan's main worry was that Sonia would just give up the rest of the championships and fly back to London. Their single-minded daughter was well capable of such an action. Eamon Coghlan predicted she would bounce back, but he did not put a time-scale on the revival. But Sonia was already thinking of the 1500 metres at the end of the week.

Eamon Coghlan has also said of O'Sullivan that you can beat her once or twice, but once she beats you, you'll never beat her again. The hallmark of her athletics career has been her single-minded determination to get back and win.

In the early days, winning was far from her mind. A career in athletics was not even considered. It wasn't even the sport itself that lured her to join Ballymore-Cobh Athletics Club. Whether it was a party, a disco, or the free food, nobody can agree, least of all Sonia herself, but it certainly was not for the racing that she went along to her first cross-country meet.

The main thing was that it was fun. Trips around Cork every weekend and stop-offs at 'the merries' in Youghal were the motivation for the young girl to stick with running. It certainly wasn't winning, because in those days she didn't win.

Names like Anita Philpott and Diane McCarthy were the promising ones. Not the tall girl from Cobh who spent as much time playing camogie and basketball as she did running. First it was Diane McCarthy who always beat Sonia into second place. Then one day she didn't anymore. Then it was Anita Philpott who took the tape first, with Sonia always running in second. Gradually Sonia moved ahead of her.

During those early rivalries, Sonia sought assistance from local athletics coach Sean Kennedy. Kennedy is the first in a triumvirate of mentors who have helped and moulded Sonia O'Sullivan, although she has always stuck rigidly to what she herself believes. Kennedy was a paternal figure in Cobh, who met the girl when she was thirteen and shaped her training for the next decade. A

Right:
Yvonne Murray
congratulates
Sonia O'Sullivan
at the World
Championships in
Stuttgart, 1993.

fax machine allowed them to communicate during the years she was at Villanova or running the international Grand Prix circuit.

Marty Stern of Villanova was her college athletics tutor in the US, a man with whom she has had disagreements, but who greatly helped the development of her international career. And thirdly, there is Kim McDonald, the London agent and former athlete who instilled in O'Sullivan a crucial self-belief and confidence, which helped her bounce back from the disappointments of Barcelona and Stuttgart. McDonald's knowledge of the international athletic scene has made him the most influential person in Sonia's career to date.

When Sean Kennedy was approached by a wiry thirteen-year-old looking for a training schedule, he prepared her one, only to see her return dissatisfied a week later, and again a week after that, always hungry for more, always looking for improvement. Kennedy took note. This girl could be good.

At that stage she was racing regularly, and she was very enthusiastic. In fact, her enthusiasm caught people's attention. She had a burning ambition to be number one in the world from a very early age, and Kennedy was highly impressed with her motivation and determination to learn. She trained every day after school on the hilly streets of Cobh, and sometimes joined the local men's club in their nightly runs, a habit she has to this day. Back then though she was training to catch up with her peers, and gradually the gaps started closing. As Anita Philpott was collecting cross-country titles, O'Sullivan rejected her other sports and concentrated on running. In 1986 she made the break, finishing in seventh place in the National Junior Cross-country Championships. She would not be beaten by Philpott again.

A year later O'Sullivan won the national schoolgirls title, the junior title, and most amazingly of all, the national senior cross-country title. Still only seventeen, Sonia was a late entrant for the championship, in which Caroline Mullen was the strong favourite. But 600 metres from the line, Sonia broke from the leaders and sprinted to the finish to take the title. The *Cork Examiner* showed her crossing the line in Killenaule, muddied, her hands entangled in her mop of hair, a look of youthful disbelief on her face. Twenty yards behind were the race favourites, Caroline Mullen, Mary Donoghue and Patricia Griffin.

That summer, athletics scout Chris Murray of Arizona University visited Cobh and took a good look at Sonia. Describing her as 'a gem', he offered her a scholarship at Arizona. He was not the only one. Five colleges in all offered her places, but in the end it was Philadelphia's Villanova and Marty Stern that claimed Sonia's talents.

Villanova has a tradition of taking on Irish athletes; Eamon Coghlan and Marcus O'Sullivan among them. For that reason, and because it is easily accessible from Ireland, Sonia opted for Philadelphia as her collegiate base. In the meantime, however, there were a few harrowing months of injury to get through.

Stress fractures are the accessories of young women in sport. Physiological development combined with training and exercise often results in injury. An ankle injury forced Sonia to miss the European Junior Championships 3000 metre final in Birmingham, and she travelled to Villanova with her leg in plaster. There she got a rude awakening to the rigours of American collegiate athletic scholarships when the Villanova coaches discarded her plaster and set her training again. Because she couldn't train properly she put on weight. It was a tough year. When she started to run in the new season of collegiate cross-country races, the stress fractures returned and despair replaced determination. Disillusioned, she returned to Cobh.

The decision that O'Sullivan then took was an indication of her spirit and never-say-die philosophy. Her will to win overcame her fear of failure, and after much consultation with her parents and Kennedy she returned to Philadelphia with a renewed resolve. She faced Marty Stern and delivered her terms. No more road running and no more stress fractures. Kennedy faxed her the training schedules from Cobh, and she stuck rigidly to her recommended diet and lifestyle to avoid injury.

Soon, Villanova and Sonia became a mutually beneficial combination. The regime was certainly tough, but she learned to stick to her guns and adapt to

Above: Back home with Mum and Dad, Mary and John, Cork airport, September 1993.

hard training schedules; self-discipline was essential. Villanova gave her an apprenticeship, where she learned her trade over five good years. On reflection, O'Sullivan and Kennedy are both of the opinion that she may have been too young when she went to the US. The advantages of the American college scholarship system are plentiful, but the athlete has to be prepared to take the knocks with the benefits. Fierce competition between students and between coaches means that rivalry breeds competition and pressure. O'Sullivan came through it well, but she may have been one of the lucky ones.

In contrast, Catherina McKiernan has refused numerous scholarships to US colleges. In McKiernan's case, she probably did the right thing. A shy person by nature, the brash competitive atmosphere of American college athletics would have been anathema to her, more at home, as she was, in Cornafean, County Cavan. It is interesting that two Irish women, of the same age and in the same sport, would have such different needs.

While at Villanova, O'Sullivan set a total of five collegiate records, one of which still stands today — her time for an indoor 5000 metres in Boston which made her a world-record holder for all of fifteen days in January 1991. It was the first real taste of success, and she was hooked. With a time of 15:17.28, she knocked a full four seconds off the Lyn Jennings' record. It did not matter that Uta Pippig stole the record from her fifteen days later; she still remains the only Irish woman ever to hold an indoor track record.

In the meantime, the full-time college athlete was adjusting well to the very different pressures of international athletics. In 1990 she represented Ireland at the West Athletic International for the small European Nations and won the 3000 metres. She participated in her first senior European Championships in Split in the summer and qualified for the final of the 3000 metres. In a manner which was to become familiar, Sonia took the lead with 800 metres to go, sending the small knot of supporters into temporary delirium. The glory was not to last, but Sonia still broke the Irish record with a time of 8:52.65.

When an athlete achieves these times and feats, it is not just the press and public who take notice. The all-important sponsors and promoters are always looking out for new attractions on the circuit, and Sonia O'Sullivan fit the bill. At first, invitations rather than appearance fees are the bonus of success, but gradually the athlete can begin to make a bit of money.

Apart from the financial rewards, international experience is something that cannot be easily attained, and every invitation from abroad was welcome. Because of television exposure, Grand Prix track events offer more money to invited athletes than cross-country meetings. A lot more people will see Sonia O'Sullivan win a 1500 metre race in Monte Carlo than will see Catherina McKiernan win the Mollusk cross-country meet in Northern Ireland.

In 1991 Sonia faced two events with contrasting fortunes: the World Student Games at Sheffield and the World Athletics Championships at Tokyo. She won a gold medal at the former and was forced to pull out of the latter because of injury. Although the 3000 metres is arguably her stronger distance, her success at Sheffield did not come over this distance. Her achilles heel, a lapse of concentration, let her Romanian rival Iulia Besliu through, and there was too much time to make up. In contrast, the 1500 metres brought her gold. Although her time was not particularly fast, she proved her worth again a week later by breaking the Irish record for the 1500 metres at Monte Carlo.

She returned home to acclamation, including an audience with President Mary Robinson at Áras an Uachtaráin.

So it came as something of a shock when Sonia withdrew from the Irish team for the World Athletics Championships. There was some talk at the time of a row between O'Sullivan and the Irish Athletics Federation, Bord Luthchleas na hEireann, but even if this were the case, injury seems to have been the real reason for not going to Tokyo.

Then it was back to Villanova to finish her degree. Due to her running commitments, O'Sullivan was 'red-shirted' by the college, which means she was given extra time to finish her final semester. But after winning her final American collegiate cross-country title, she returned home for Christmas and decided to run in the international meet at Mollusk near Belfast. Unbeknownst to her, participation in such a race was prohibited by Villanova's 'red-shirt' rule and effectively ended her student days.

Ireland was now eager to see a clash of its two female athletics stars, O'Sullivan and McKiernan, at Mollusk. While O'Sullivan had been busy across the Atlantic, McKiernan had quietly won two successive senior national cross-country titles. Mollusk was to prove her ability on the grass. The Cavan girl won, with O'Sullivan finishing well down the pack in sixteenth place. Despite showing such a lack of form, Sonia was picked along with McKiernan for the World Cross-country Championships in Boston in March.

That race, in snowy muddy conditions, was a triumph for the Irish girls, with McKiernan taking the silver behind Lyn Jennings and O'Sullivan finishing in seventh. It was unprecedented that two Irish women would finish in the top ten of a world championship final, but it had happened and in appalling conditions. Many track athletes run cross-country during the winter, and there is nothing wrong with a track athlete running cross-country as long as they finish in March — which is precisely what O'Sullivan did in 1992.

She returned to the track to prepare her build-up for the Barcelona Olympics. In May, O'Sullivan at last broke her nine-minute personal barrier for the 3000 metres. More importantly, just over a month later she demolished her own Irish record with a time of 8:39.63. It was the second fastest time of the year for the 3000 metres, and O'Sullivan was now a household name at the summer Grand Prix meets. It was at one of these meets that she had the infamous encounter with the Moroccan runner Hassiba Boulmerka. During a race in Lille, Boulmerka, never one to bow easily to an opponent, tripped O'Sullivan while jostling for space on the track. Later that summer the feisty Moroccan became Olympic champion in the 1500 metres. A year later she was to prove an unlikely ally to O'Sullivan in the final of the 3000 metres at the World Championships in Stuttgart.

Barcelona awaited, and O'Sullivan spent the summer at home in Cork before joining the Irish track and field team at a pre-Olympics summer camp in the south of France. On reflection, she believes that staying in Ireland may have been a mistake. Hype was building up about the Olympics, and at every turn she was being asked about Barcelona. She did not have the peace she needed to prepare mentally.

Barcelona was not the luxurious Olympic village that many expected. While the city basked in the splendour of the occasion, the athletes baked in the sweltering heat, in accommodation which was not air-conditioned. It was hardly surprising that many athletes, including the American basketball 'Dream Team', opted for separate, air-conditioned quarters away from the village. It is a fact of an international athlete's life that accommodation and conditions at major championships tend to be spartan.

Sonia's 3000 metre heat took place on Friday, August 1, the last of the three qualifying heats. She was so nervous in the hours leading up to the race that she had to eat plain rice with a bit of salt — she couldn't stomach anything else. She was shaky and disorientated. She whiled away the hours leading up to the race by watching MTV and nervously trying to write postcards. Three hours before the race she showered and changed in preparation for the track.

With the other runners she watched the first two heats, conscious of the importance that times would play in their own qualification chances. The first heat was slow, the second faster, putting pressure on Sonia to finish in the top three. For the first 200 metres of her race she seemed stymied. Then she tripped slightly and grabbed the singlet of the runner in front of her to steady herself. The athlete's number came away in her hand, and if she had not held on so tightly she could have gone down. It was at that moment that her mother Mary chose to go down to the barrier and take a photo of her daughter. As she watched Sonia stumble she nearly ran out of the stadium with fright. One fall can ruin many ambitions, as Mary Decker-Slaney will testify.

But she won her heat, awakening an excitement in the Irish public. Here was an Irish woman competing at the Olympics who seemed to have a real chance of a medal. The nation stared at their television sets on that Sunday night. Sonia's brother was in the crowd at Feíle in Semple Stadium when the race was shown live. The country held its breath.

As the finalists in the women's 3000 metres gathered on the track, Sonia became aware of the Irish tricolours around the stadium. Forcing herself to concentrate, she looked away from a banner with her name on it and jogged to warm up. Then the athletes were called to the line for the start of the race. Sonia looked up above the stadium walls and saw the Olympic flame. 'I remember thinking, "Oh my God, this is the Olympics".'

Then she looked up into the crowd one last time, and her eyes met her father's. 'I just happened to glance into the crowd and who did I see only my father. It was weird. Our eyes just met. I mean there were a thousand people there, but he was the one I picked out. We smiled.'

The gun went and the race was on, slow for the first few laps. Alison Wyeth moved up front, still fairly slow. Sonia stayed with the pack, planning to go for it with 150 metres left. With 500 to go, Yvonne Murray pulled away. Sonia followed her as planned. Suddenly Murray faded and O'Sullivan found herself in front on her own. It was too soon. She didn't want the lead on the last bend, but that is where she found herself. She started looking for shadows, and then Romanova and Dorovskiyh sped past. Sonia looked to her left. Wrong. Angela Chalmers came through on her right, and as she passed, Sonia could not react quickly enough. She crossed the line, thinking she had blown it.

Her father, John O'Sullivan sat with his head in his hands and cried. Sonia left the track and was then told to take a drug test. After a short while she realised that, while it was an opportunity gone, it was not the end. She met up with her parents before returning to the Olympic village.

Rather than do the traditional 'running down' after the race on the warmup track, O'Sullivan jogged back to the Olympic village with Kim McDonald. It was an unwinding experience and perhaps a bonding one. McDonald listened as the Irish woman talked out her feelings about the race, getting the frustration of fourth place out of her system.

'Kim gave me a lot of confidence, just in a one-to-one discussion sense and I felt it was valuable,' she said later. 'Of course, Sean had given me a great deal in the build-up to Barcelona but I suppose I was in more contact with Kim and he did have the experience of high pressure races.'

Eventually she settled on what she felt about her fourth place in the Olympic 3000 metres final, disregarding the expectations of others. 'What other people think I should have done ultimately doesn't matter. Because they weren't on the track making the decisions. I didn't run badly. I just ended up in the wrong place at the wrong time.'

O'Sullivan was entered in the 1500 metres, but the experience in the 3000 metre final had taken more out of her than she thought. She finished in fifth place in her slow heat, but qualified for the semifinal. She looked leaden in the race and finished well down, in eleventh place. She had injured her ankle prior to the 1500 metre heat, but there had also been a little psychological damage. This, however, would heal quickly.

When the Irish Olympic team returned on a euphoric flight to Dublin Airport, the cameras and press focussed on the medal winners McCullough and Carruth. At the rear of the plane, the rest of the team alighted, tired and smiling at the reception being afforded their team-mates. A notable absentee was O'Sullivan. The Cobh woman had serious business to attend to: a Grand Prix blitz in the next few weeks during which she broke the existing Irish records for the 1500, 3000, the mile and the 5000 metres. She also beat her main rivals along the way, including those who had passed her in Barcelona.

The races were set up by her agent Kim McDonald, who by now was playing a much stronger role in her career. Originally involved with O'Sullivan through her Reebok contract, McDonald was now handling her appearances and race fees.

O'Sullivan won the overall Grand Prix prize of $10,000. She was chosen to run for Europe at the Athletics World Cup, but she declined, returning home before travelling to Philadelphia to her winter base.

She trained through the winter, but an injury forced her to reconsider her entry into the World Cross-country Championships at Bilbao in March. On the advice of many, including Kennedy, she decided to withdraw, in the interest of her forthcoming track season and the World Athletics Championships at Stuttgart. Unable to run, she swam and lifted weights. She was determined to keep in shape, so she started running again. She felt a real purpose about it, a great hunger. The World Championships in Stuttgart became her priority.

O'Sullivan ran a series of American road races in March, preparing for her return to the European track circuit in May. In the meantime, Catherina

McKiernan took a magnificent silver at Bilbao, while Sonia watched the race on television. She returned to Ireland in March. That summer of 1993 she notched up the Grand Prix points and victories: Zurich, Monte Carlo, Oslo, Berlin, Brussels, Crystal Palace. Then Stuttgart, and the silver which brought out the biggest smile of all.

She started with first place in the 1500 metres in Granada in Spain on May 29. Two wins at 1500 and 3000 metres in Holland were followed by a fifth place in an unfamiliar distance, a 1000 metre race in Lille, France.

Then came the Bislett Games in Oslo on July 10. The venue has been the scene of many new world records and attempts over the years, and it is almost inspirational to an athlete who harbours any wish to write her name in the history books. Sonia was no exception.

She aimed for the 3000 metre record, but the pacemaker or 'rabbit' was not on form. Yet Sonia won in a time of 8.28.74, prompting the great Gretta Weits to exclaim, 'Look at the time, look at the time!'

Wins followed in the 1500 metres at Nice and Copenhagen, and in the 3000 metres in Zurich. Sonia came second in the 1500 at Monte Carlo on August 7, but she describes it as one of her most satisfying races; she had gone under four minutes for the first time at the distance — 3.59.60 was the magic number.

All summer O'Sullivan based herself in London. She had excellent training facilities and was able to concentrate fully on her form. As an athlete, O'Sullivan was beginning to develop a new determination and will to succeed which seemed to be even stronger than before. Her single-minded focus on her running career meant that she began to be far more careful of what she said to the media; she was not letting anything away this time. Being in London meant that there was far less home-grown pressure on her. She was away from the hype of Ireland and had Kim McDonald close by to advise her.

As Stuttgart beckoned she was firm favourite to take the 3000 metre gold, in spite of news of fast times from China. A great deal of scepticism greeted these times, and once it was confirmed that Wang Junxia was not entered in the 3000 metres, many felt that Sonia was safe. Junxia was the only athlete to have run faster than the Cork woman at the 3000 metres in 1993. There were other Chinese certainly, and Sonia was well aware of them, but there remained a prevailing attitude, of 'what we have not seen cannot hurt'.

At that point Sonia's entire race focus was on the 3000 metres; she would not confirm whether she would run the 1500. The 3000 was her distance, her race.

The week would be an emotional roller coaster, as she came an agonising fourth in the 3000 metres and picked herself up to take the silver in the 1500 metres a week later. It was an extraodinary performance and spoke worlds of what O'Sullivan had achieved in terms of building her own confidence. That fourth place behind the three Chinese would have crushed many an athlete, but O'Sullivan bounced back. Her father, John O'Sullivan described the week succinctly: 'She lifted us on Saturday, she put us in the gutter on Monday, she wouldn't talk to us for two days, she lifted us again on Friday and we haven't come down since Sunday.'

O'Sullivan started the week in very relaxed form. She arrived at her first press conference on a mountain bike wearing denim shorts and a tee shirt. She smiled and posed for photographs beside the Irish tricolour. Her heat went well, and she won easily, ahead of the Chinese athlete Qu. The general consensus was that, although impressive, the Chinese were tactically erratic. Much was made of their disciplined training runs, under the guidance of their coach Ma Jungren.

Sonia prepared for the final on the Monday. She kept to herself and didn't see her parents. She rang them in the afternoon and told them that she felt good. Going into the 3000 metre final, Sonia was thinking about the gold medal. She believed she was going to win, and she had no reason to feel afraid or intimidated.

The race progressed without incident until the last 700 metres. Yvonne Murray was between the Chinese and Sonia. By the time that Murray and Sonia reacted, the Chinese had opened up a considerable gap, all in the space of a hundred metres.

After the disappointing 3000, the Irish team manager, Fr Liam Kelleher, banned media communication with Sonia until Friday's 1500 heat. He also gave her free reign to do as she wished during the interim. The boredom of the championship village can be stifling at times, especially if an athlete has a lot of time to kill. She kept her own routine and worked out in her head what she planned to do. Now she had nothing to lose.

During those few days, Scotland's Yvonne Murray called over to the Irish camp to sympathise with Sonia on her disappointment. It was a warm and gracious gesture by the Scot, who had spent most of the summer trailing O'Sullivan in Grand Prix races. Fr Liam Kelleher presented Murray with a bottle of cream liqueur to show the team's appreciation.

O'Sullivan's 1500 metre heat was on Friday evening. She was in good form, and showed it in the race. As she ran in to win the heat, a Chinese athlete tried to come in on her inside. O'Sullivan moved over and with the slightest little nudge, forced her back. She took the tape smiling.

The 1500 metre final was on Sunday afternoon. The O'Sullivan family and the Irish fans tried to gather in the same spot — in front of the Chinese coaches. But they had been beaten to it by Hassiba Boulmerka's Moroccan contingent who had positioned themselves right in front of Ma Jungren and his fellow coaches. They manically waved their flags up and down and created a rumpus to try and drown out any shouted directions.

Every time the athletes approached the bend where the Chinese coaches sat, the Moroccans leapt up and down in front of them as the athletes looked up for signals. At this point, Sonia was completely unaware of such shenanigans, but she had decided in her mind that she was going to win a medal. With 700 metres to go, the Chinese made their move. O'Sullivan hesitated slightly, but this time she was more prepared. Liu broke away, but behind her the planned Chinese slipstream did not follow. Yi Lu at first chased at the bell, but then began to weaken as Boulmerka made her move. The Moroccan was like a terrier on the track, nudging, grunting and spitting, trying to disrupt the Chinese rhythm. O'Sullivan followed in her wake, happy that the former Olympic champion was taking on the hard work. Boulmerka moved into second, pulling O'Sullivan into third. The German crowd rose, sensing an upset of the Chinese.

Suddenly O'Sullivan found her extra strength and passed Boulmerka between the last two bends. She was not going to catch Liu, but she resisted a counter-attack by the Moroccan and took the silver, to her obvious joy and acclamation from the crowd. John O'Sullivan had dropped his stop watch, and Mary had her head in her hands (she missed the entire last lap). The Irish fans were ecstatic. John struggled down to hand his daughter a flag. Some Dubliners got there first, and Sonia jogged her lap of honour with a tricolour aloft in her hand. The German crowd gave her an extraordinary reception, which bordered on the embarrassing. Their xenophobic reaction to Chinese success meant that Sonia O'Sullivan was proclaimed as some kind of saviour.

'Emotionally it was something which embraced everything you dream about,' she said afterwards. 'The finish gave me a feeling like never before but then the lap of honour was the real high for me. It was difficult to take it all in and I suppose it underlines the situation where a medal in a major championship is so special and why missing out on one in Barcelona was so difficult to take at the time.'

In Croke Park in Dublin a message of her medal flashed up on the screen, and Dublin and Derry fans cheered as one.

Stuttgart over, it was back to London and a sense of anticlimax. There was also the little matter of the Grand Prix season and the rest of the big European meetings. Berlin beckoned the following Friday night, and O'Sullivan decided to stay in London and prepare for the race. Cork's homecoming had to be delayed.

If she and Kim McDonald had any worries about her losing form after such a high, they need not have worried. She ran a stormer of a 5000 metres, and was on her own for the last two laps, obliterating a world-class field. Brussels was next and a gold bar prize for winning the 'big four' awaited. Yvonne Murray passed her briefly on the last lap, but then O'Sullivan rallied and took the lead, the tape, and the title. The two athletes embraced and once again Murray had to take second place to the Irish woman.

Crystal Palace was the venue for the Grand Prix final. O'Sullivan was well in the running for the overall women's prize for the best running of the season. She ran in the 3000 metres and beat Murray after exchanging the lead for some time. The win confirmed her position as Grand Prix champion. Two days later, O'Sullivan ran and won the Princes Street Mile in Edinburgh. She easily beat

Yvonne Murray on the Scotswoman's home turf. Boulmerka was also well down the ranks.

With the season effectively over, Sonia had one more trip abroad. She travelled to Japan to run the 5000 metres in the Fukijara Super Invitational Meeting. En route, she and Kim McDonald visited Hong Kong, coming as close as was possible to the Chinese border and her rivals. She won the Tokyo race, almost on her own, and that was the end of the dramatic season.

She returned to Cork and a postponed homecoming. Cobh awaited its heroine while Sonia received her tenth Jury's of Cork Sports Star Award in Cork city. Hundreds were gathered in Cobh in anticipation of her return appearance. She arrived with the Cobh fire brigade leading the procession. The whole town was decked in tricolours. 'I brought back a silver medal but you know there is still one step to go,' she told the cheering throng when she arrived.

Within the year, the precious gold would be hers, but 1994 brought with it the customary problems which face a top-class athlete. Sonia, based in London and running regularly with McDonald's Kenyan athletes, found herself with an achilles tendon injury that would not go away. Running in Cork's Mardyke, where she was home to collect yet another award, she headed out for a run. Her leg would not react and trouble loomed.

Her chances of running in the World Cross-country Championships in Bucharest along with Catherina McKiernan looked bad. Hopes of competing receded after she pulled out of a cross-country Grand Prix meeting in Seville. As she had not gone to Mollusk, Seville had been anticipated as the venue for the first meeting between McKiernan and O'Sullivan since their run in the snow in Boston in 1992.

The injury was increasingly worrying. With an eye on the rest of the season, and particularly the European Championships, O'Sullivan and McDonald looked for a resolution. Gerard Hartmann, physical therapist and former Limerick jeweller, proved to be the recipe for recovery. O'Sullivan travelled to his clinic in Florida for treatment. The World Cross-country Championships were abandoned, and once again O'Sullivan watched while her Irish team-mate collected her third silver medal. Hartmann worked on O'Sullivan's tired limb and discovered that she was close to completely shredding a tendon, something which could have caused permanent damage. He recommended complete rest.

Rest and treatment proved the cure. O'Sullivan returned to the track in April, and despite her absence from the competitive cross-country circuit, she appeared as eager and as capable as ever. Her friendly rivalry was renewed with Yvonne Murray, who unfortunately found herself in the old position of following her Irish rival's back.

The new year brought far greater rewards for the Cobh athlete than many deemed possible. O'Sullivan returned to the Grand Prix circuit, where she had excelled in 1993 and was clearly comfortable. She enoyed the compact European stadiums where the knowledgeable crowds appreciated their athletics, and world-record attempts were common. Oslo, Zurich and Berlin were the customary venues for such records, but Sonia would write her name into the record books that year in Edinburgh.

No Irish athlete had ever held an IAAF outdoor world record, and even Dr Pat O'Callaghan's hammer-throwing exploits sixty years ago were not recorded officially. In Edinburgh, O'Sullivan ran in the 2000 metres, not strictly speaking a championship distance but still a race with a record attached. Prior to the race she felt she had a chance at the record, particularly after a run with Marcus O'Sullivan the week before. Her times were very fast, and finishing up the session with two laps of sixty-two seconds apiece, she knew she was onto something. And so she was, as she clocked a history-making 5.25:36, a full 3.31 seconds faster than the old record.

The success spurred her on. She continued on the Grand Prix circuit, advised constantly by her close mentor and agent Kim McDonald. She won the 1500 metres in Stockholm, the same meeting at which Catherina McKiernan chopped a massive forty-one seconds off her Irish record for the 10,000 metres. The Irish women were running Europe.

July 15 brought Crystal Palace and O'Sullivan's favourite distance — the 3000 metres. An attempt at the world record was not in question, as the Chinese had pushed the parameters too far for an athlete with even O'Sullivan's improvement curve. But the European record was there for the taking. Maria Akara of Sweden set the pace, but by the fourth lap Sonia felt it needed pushing so she moved to the front, followed as usual by Yvonne Murray. The bell sounded at 7.19:63. O'Sullivan needed to clock a sixty-three second final lap. She produced 62.02 and the record was hers.

Wins in Nice and Oslo followed, and O'Sullivan continued to run in European races planned by herself and McDonald. Observers and reporters expressed concern that she might be overdoing it with the European Championship just a month away. Their fears and warnings were heightened when she lost in Monte Carlo, and twice in the St Petersburg Goodwill Games – though in one of her Goodwill Games losses, she set an Irish record for the 800 metres.

O'Sullivan herself took note of the losses and announced that she would only run in the 3000 in Helsinki. In St Petersburg she had been beaten tactically by a few Russian athletes, among them the forty-two-year-old mother Petrakova. Cries went up that O'Sullivan could only run against the clock, and that her medal propsects were in danger. The Cobh athlete meanwhile set her sights on gold in the 3000.

'I was so completely focussed on winning the gold that nothing could distract me,' she said later. 'I just ignored whatever people were saying because ultimately it's up to me, and it doesn't matter what anybody else thinks, it's what I think and do that matters. Anyway, I think I proved them wrong by winning that medal, don't you?'

Above: Sonia O'Sullivan (left) and Yvonne Murray (right) with their gold and silver medals in the European Championships in Helsinki.

Sonia's performance at Helsinki did indeed prove her critics wrong. She easily won her heat, and it was apparent after the two qualifying races that the only real threat to her would come from Scotland's Yvonne Murray, the reigning European champion and O'Sullivan's great rival.

When Murray won her gold medal four years previously in Split, twenty-year-old O'Sullivan had trailed home a disappointed eleventh. In Helsinki it was a completely different animal who took to the track in a green singlet. She had won a silver medal in the World Athletics Championships in the 1500 metres, had been the leading woman middle distance runner in the Grand Prix series in 1993, and had just broken the world record for the 2000 metres. Murray may have beeen the reigning champion, but that did not count for much to O'Sullivan.

Sonia planned the race perfectly. She was prepared to stay with Murray for as long as possible until she felt that the moment was right; her kick could take her to the tape. That is exactly how it happened. On the first lap, Anita Philpott, the Cork woman who had consistently beat O'Sullivan in her teens, helped her team-mate by setting the pace. Murray had anticipated this, and when Philpott fell back at the beginning of the third lap the wiry Scot took over. O'Sullivan saw her intention and joined Murray at the front. Soon the two were alone, leaving Britain's Alison Wyeth and the fancied Russian Lyudmilla Borislova in their wake.

It was a classic battle — Ireland versus Great Britain on the track and the Irish in the crowd cheering O'Sullivan on. Sonia was as happy as she could be. She knew she had her kick in reserve, and if she could stick with the tiring Murray she would win.

She burst ahead with less than a lap to go. Murray was unable to respond, and the Cobh woman strengthened her stride and ran the last 200 metres in a rapid time of 29.46 seconds. This time there was no looking back, no glance over the shoulder. She knew the gold was hers. 'The last time I looked over my shoulder, it cost me the bronze medal and I dared not risk it again,'she said. 'But I guessed from the reaction of the crowd that I was away on my own and the title was mine at last.'

Her arms shot in the air as she crossed the finishing line. Beginning her lap of honour, she searched the crowd for her father and was amazed when he appeared beside her with a tricolour clasped in his hand. The pair embraced and photographers gathered to capture the moment. At last she did the customary lap of honour, the tricolour draped over her shoulders. It was Ireland's first gold medal in track athletics since Eamon Coghlan's victory in the 5000 metres in the 1983 World Athletics Championships in the same stadium.

Back in Dublin, Coghlan and Bill O'Herlihy were doing their studio analysis in RTE. They had been joined for the European Championships by John Treacy, who had proved to be a natural on the screen as well as the track. Basking in O'Sullivan's victory, Treacy and Coghlan hoped she might go for the 1500 metres and the unique double. Since O'Sullivan's decision to enter only the 3000 metres there had been speculation in the Irish media that she had grown scared after her loss in St Petersburg. There were also mutterings about Kim McDonald's influence over her, that perhaps he was over-running her in the pursuit of money and not her better interests.

In Helsinki, George Hamilton interviewed the breathless O'Sullivan, and Coghlan suggested she go for the double gold. But Sonia stuck to her plan and left with McDonald the day after she received her medal to return to London and prepare for Zurich and an assault on the mile record.

The Zurich meeting, one of the 'big four' of the summer Grand Prix events, has always been a major occasion in athletics, but the 1994 meet had an extra incentive for the invited athletes. The sponsors had offered a bonus of $100,000 for a new women's world mile record, and O'Sullivan was going for it. The 'rabbits' were set up, and it did not go unnoticed that the Russian athlete

Podkopayeva, who had defeated O'Sullivan in St Petersburg, was one of them. As it happened, when the evening came it was obvious no records would be set. Torrential rain and a very strong wind turned the night's races into a lottery. Sonia was beaten into second place by her old rival Hassiba Boulmerka. Her arms and legs felt very heavy — lactic acid in the system, nature's way of telling her to stop running and rest. The loss in Zurich meant that the four bars of gold, offered to athletes who won their events at the big four meets, were beyond her reach.

The final event of the Grand Prix season was in Paris on September 3. Despite her recent loss of form, O'Sullivan was still in with a shot at the overall women's prize, though at this stage it seemed unlikely; her fatigue was palpable. She was entered in the 5000 metres (the 3000 metres in Stuttgart was the last time that the race was run over such a distance), but there was an extra dimension to the race — Catherina McKiernan was also entered.

O'Sullivan and McKiernan had not raced against each other since the World Cross-country Championships in Boston in 1992. Ireland watched in anticipation. For a clearly exhausted O'Sullivan, pride and money were at stake. McKiernan needed to erase the memory of disappointment at Helsinki with a solid performance. Her third place in the 5000 metres at the Berlin Grand Prix had restored some of the Cavan woman's confidence, and she wanted another good run to tie up the end of the track season.

O'Sullivan was competing with the heptathlon and long jump athlete Jackie Joyner-Kersey of the US and high hurdler Svetlana Dimitrova. The odds favoured the sprinter and the jumper; it is much more difficult to make up points for the competition in a long race.

O'Sullivan broke for the front from the first lap, clear in her intention of giving the competition her best shot. At first it seemed that nobody would follow her, then from the pack came another woman in the blue Reebok running strip. Catherina McKiernan chased O'Sullivan and then shadowed her until 1000 metres from the end. For a moment, McKiernan hovered on the shoulder in an apparent announcement that she was about to take on the Cork woman. However, O'Sullivan awoke to the almost audacious threat from her team-mate and she shot off for home.

Sonia won the race in a time of 15 minutes and 12.94 seconds, but it was not enough to catch Joyner-Kersey in the competition for the Grand Prix winner. She finished third overall and collected a cheque for £20,000 for her efforts.

After Paris, the season was effectively over. Losses at Sheffield and Crystal Palace confirmed her exhaustion. But for Sonia O'Sullivan, running is all she knows and all she wants. The money piles up, but she keeps going anyway. In Dublin the following October, she collected a special presentation from the BLE, where she confessed that a week after the season was over she didn't know what to do with herself.

The early months and winter of 1995 brought for Sonia a change in destination and climate facilitated by her sister Gillian's sojourn in Australia. And so, the snows of Philadelphia, so long her winter base were swapped for the sunny beaches and temperate weather of the southern hemisphere.

The change in destination clearly suited the Cobh athlete and she resolved to go there in the winter of 1996 also. However, even if she found her training and lifestyle suited her perfectly, on returning to basecamp at Teddington, an injury crisis once again reared its head. Gerard Hartmann, the ex-pat Irish man based in Florida was once again called upon to put matters right, but it was too late to rectify the situation in time for the World Cross-country Championships. As Sonia O'Sullivan watched Catherina McKiernan pick up her fourth silver medal in a row at Durham, she could only reflect that it had been four years since she herself had been able to challenge for the title; every year injury got in the way.

But Sonia can also claim to be lucky in that those unfortunate injuries have not interrupted her highly successful and high-profile track career. Sonia was back, and running faster times than ever after a month or two, and soon it was Catherina who had to suffer and sit out the World Track and Field Championships in Gothenburg.

When O'Sullivan returned to training, the word got around that she was notching up incredibly fast times with the Kenyans in London. She had recovered well under Hartmann's guidance, and had found the use of aquatherapy especially helpful.

However, such talk of speed was all very well until you got on the track. An early season 1500 metres race at Crystal Palace in London was a rude awakening, when Britain's Kelly Holmes sped past her on the final stretch to take the tape. But as Eamon Coghlan had said, you'll beat her once but you won't beat her again. O'Sullivan admitted that she wasn't yet up to scratch but did not panic. She chose her track races carefully, and unlike the previous summer, when it seemed to all observers that she had overraced, she took things calmly and raced with confidence and style for the rest of the summer.

The first of the 'big four'; Oslo, proved to be almost an anticlimax. Running in the 5000 metres, O'Sullivan took the lead with a lap to go, and there she stayed, her opponents stringing out behind her, like a dissipating wake. The form looked good for Gothenburg, particularly since the formerly dominant Chinese appeared to have vanished into the athletics history books. There was always a suspicion however, that they would appear at the World Championships.

A 1500 metre race in Monte Carlo should have been something of a warmup for Gothenburg, as it was O'Sullivan's last race before the Championships, but it was the way she won it that sent shivers of anticipation across the world of athletics. O'Sullivan was left to run effectively on her own, after Hassiba Boulmerka of Algeria fell in the early stages. With over a lap to go, the lithe

Irish woman broke away on a solo. The win seemed facile, and she looked like she was strolling down the home straight. When she crossed the line, the crowd were stunned at the time. She had run two seconds under the four minute 'barrier', smashing her own Irish record, and setting the fastest time in the world for the distance in 1995.

The question now was, would Sonia opt to go for the golden double in Gothenburg? Timing was the crucial factor in this competition, and as the shorter race was before the 5000 metres, a conservative maturity prevailed. Again, lessons of the past had been learnt, and Sonia O'Sullivan was after the gold at her favourite distance; the 5000 metres. As she said herself, ''Why go for two, when I just want to be world champion?'

As she observed Hassiba Boulmerka win the gold in the 1500 metre at Gothenburg, O'Sullivan did admit that she felt a twinge, that she could have done it. However, that was for another day, and she would prove a point to Boulmerka later in the season.

Ireland awaited their golden girl meanwhile, and John and Mary travelled out to support her. Arriving on the Monday of the competition, O'Sullivan was booked into a top hotel by her sponsors Reebok. No more the congested accommodation for the run-of-the-mill athletes who gasped without air conditioning. The 'Dream Team' breathed rarified calming surroundings.

The heat of the 5000 metres was on Thursday. She made light work of it, accelerating magnificently around the last bend to stretch easily towards the tape. The race was run early in the sunny morning and it awoke a shiver of anticipation in the sleepy Swedish crowd.

The media gathered to pounce, but O'Sullivan kept her utterances to a minimum. Yes, she was quite calm, thank you. No, she wasn't particulalry worried about Fernando Ribiera of Portugal. The latter had broken the world record for the 5000 metres earlier in the summer, and had won the gold medal in the 10,000 metres in Gothenburg that week. She was now making it clear that she wanted O'Sullivan's scalp, but the Irish woman remained nonplussed.

Saturday evening, O'Sullivan lined up looking calm. Three years previously she may have watched the crowd, she might have noticed the fans and flags, but not now. This was focussing as never before. The gun went, and the slight Romanian Szabo streaked into a fast lead. It was a strange start to an odd race. Quick, quick, slow, and tactics. After the initial surge by Szabo, things got congested in the pack, and for a minute Ireland held its breath as Sonia seemed to trip. A long jumper was to blame, and for a surreal moment, Sonia glared at her Kenyan opponent, thinking she was at fault, before concentrating on getting back into the real event; the race.

The crowd waited for Ribeiro to make her move, and sure enough, with 600 metres to go, the Portuguese sped into the lead. It was never going to succeed, however, as Sonia O'Sullivan simply sat on her shoulder waiting to make the move that really counted. As John Treacy said later, 'You knew at that moment she was going to win'.

With 200 metres to go, O'Sullivan's long limbs finally started to lift from the track and the acceleration was instant. In seconds, Ribeiro was a distant memory, and the only question was, how much would she win it by. She streaked ahead alone on the home straight, never looking back, never chasing shadows, and took the line. This year she did not throw her arms in the air. It was more of a sense of achievement and relief as she bent over regaining her breath; the gold was hers at last.

John O'Sullivan stood at the track waiting to embrace his daughter. It was the picture that was to adorn just about every European newspaper the following morning. They hugged, and she continued on her way around the track, accepting the applause of the crowd and the many Irish supporters. She did not carry a flag, something that prompted a few phone calls from the valley of the squinting windows back home. She ran, she smiled, she hugged, she signed autographs and she even raced the championship's mascot. She looked like she could do it all again.

'It's deadly exciting here,' she laughed to George Hamilton as he spoke to her on the side of the track. And so it was. Later that evening, she received the gold medal, and the tricolour was hoisted over Gothenburg, thus sealing the fact that she is Ireland's greatest living athlete.

The flag controversy was actually more of a storm in a teacup, and Sonia was visibly upset by it the following day. She broke down in an RTE sport interview, and later did a piece for news which deliberately mentioned the 'support of the Irish people'. Obviously she felt that she had to do it, but that was not the case. O'Sullivan does not owe Ireland anything in reality. Everything the country gets from her is a bonus. She left to train in the US at the age of seventeen and has lived abroad ever since. Frankly, people should be glad that she runs for Ireland at all, looking at the long jumper Fiona May, who left Britain to compete for her husband's country; Italy. Sonia explained later that she was looking for a flag with a pole, and then as the lap went on she didn't know which one to take, and so didn't take any.

Whether it is an excuse or not, it doesn't matter. She wears the vest of Ireland, and has raised the tricolour over victory rostrums in three international championships. She also makes it clear that Gothenburg was just a dress rehearsal for Atlanta.

She spoke later about the fact that she did not look back on the home stretch. 'I kept trying to go faster and faster to get to the finishing line. The thing is that for some reason I will never look back. No reason. I just don't do it.'

There is of course a reason, but it is typical of her focussed mind that she has blotted it out. The reason is Barcelona 1992, and the split second when a glance behind cost her the bronze medal. She has learnt from that and from every other race that she has done, like a true pro, like an athlete with a one-track mind.

Above: Sonia wins gold in the 5000 metres at the World Athletics Championships, 1995.

A week after Gothenburg, the lingering question about the feasability of the 1500 – 5000 metre double was answered. In Cologne, O'Sullivan beat the newly-crowned World Champion Hassiba Boulmerka by two seconds; a most satisfactory victory, thus setting the agenda for Atlanta 1996.

In terms of money, Sonia O'Sullivan is a very bankable product. In 1993 she earned approximately £200,000 between race winnings and sponsorship. In 1994, she maximised her earning potential on the Grand Prix circuit by winning a European gold medal and of course in 1995, she became one of the most sought-after female athletes on the international circuit. The realities of commerce are that male athletes still command higher fees on the Grand Prix circuit, but Sonia O'Sullivan is one of the highest paid of the women.

O'Sullivan has progressed from being the eager amateur in Cobh, to Ireland's first female million dollar athlete.

As a resident of the UK, Sonia plays 25 per cent tax, and her agent Kim McDonald receives 15 per cent of all earnings.

SONIA O'SULLIVAN : THE MILLION DOLLAR BREAKDOWN FOR 1995.

Monte Carlo Grand Prix Final;	
overall women's prize; a potential of :	$100,000
(For winning her own event; the 5000 metres)	
a potential of :	30,000
(The Golden Four 21 Bars of gold:	
a potential of:	250,000
Realistic winnings; a quarter share of above:	65,000
Winnings for the 8 Grand Prix One series:	
(10,000 each) Totalling for the 8:	80,000
Reebok sponsorship ($100, 000 over two years):	50,000
Reebok bonus for World Championship gold:	75,000
Heinz sponsorship:	20,000
World Championship Mercedes (value):	65,000
Appearance fees for Grand Prix races: (15,000 each)	
Totalling for the 8 meetings:	200,000
Appearance fees for smaller races,	
e.g. Gateshead, Moscow:	10,000
Cospoir grant:	35,000
TOTAL POTENTIAL INCOME	
FOR 1995 TRACK SEASON:	$955,000

Sonia O'Sullivan is probably Ireland's most successful athlete ever. Her name is synonymous internationally with success. At the age of twenty-five she still has a long way to go and potentially, she can keep running at middle distance level until her mid-thirties. One thing is for sure, she is going to be around for a long time to come.

Appearances on news programmes and television shows are the trappings of sporting success in Ireland. Sonia O'Sullivan is not too comfortable with the fuss and ceremony of awards. She freely admits that she finds the acclamation on returning to Irish soil a little hard to take. She yearns to be anonymous, and that is why her London base suits her so much.

It is close to home, but not too close.

She has the Kenyans to train with, the facilities, and the support and advice of Kim McDonald. At the end of 1993 she bought an apartment in London, and put down roots for the first time since leaving Cobh as a seventeen-year-old student.

Philadelphia has been left behind. O'Sullivan keeps counsel with only a few people: her sister Gillian, Kim McDonald, her Kenyan training partners and, when she is in America, Marcus O'Sullivan and Frank O'Meara. She has lived as an international athlete since she was a teenager, and the Irish home is quite far away from her daily life. O'Sullivan has in many ways grown more introverted as the years have gone on, the result of hours of training and racing on her own.

Many Irish people find her apparent distance hard to understand. In 1992 she appeared on *The Late Late Show* and seemed reticent, smiling at an obviously nervous Gay Byrne. Reporters often joke about the loneliness of interviewing the long distance runner. Sonia O'Sullivan knows herself. She wants to be the best, and she is not finished yet. In many respects she is the same fifteen-year-old who came to Sean Kennedy a decade ago and declared her intentions: 'I want to be the best in the world.'

Left: Sonia and the gold medal for the 5000 metres at the World Athletics Championships, 1995.

Angela Downey

Angela Downey was born in 1957 in Ballyragget, county Kilkenny. She is the holder of twelve All-Ireland Senior County Championship medals, eight National League medals, and five All-Ireland Club Championship medals. In 1985 she won the Gradam Taillte, the first person to win the Camogie Superstar title on more than one occasion. Her exploits on the camogie pitch, whether for Callan, Maynooth, St Paul's, Lisdowney or Kilkenny, are legendary. Soon her daughter Katie will begin to appreciate what a mother she has. Angela's father, Shem, won an All-Ireland senior hurling medal for Kilkenny in 1947 and a junior All-Ireland medal in 1946. Angela Downey won a Texaco Sportstar award in 1986, and she previously won four Bank of Ireland awards for Player of the Year. In 1994, Angela and Ann Downey won the All-Ireland Club final with Lisdowney. It is not often that a Kilkenny hurler can be said to be overshadowed by his daughters.

~

'My dad? Proud? Oh, he'd make a show of you,' laughs Angela Downey.

Camogie is a sister sport of hurling and Gaelic football, with all the passion but little of the glamour. Though it has been a sport without frills, where the women change in ditches and vans and make their own sandwiches for the post-match meal, sponsorship is at last beginning to help. In 1994 Kilkenny camogie was boosted by the sponsorship of Avonmore Creameries, and in 1995 Bord na Gaeilge are sponsoring the All-Ireland Camogie Championship, the first time the competition has been financed by a sponsor.

For the most part, however, talent and dedication keep the sport ticking over, and the teams that reach the All-Ireland finals on the fourth Sunday in September, like all camogie teams, are engaged in a labour of love. The tickets are never sold out in advance, the attendance is usually in the region of 6,000, and the match will receive a lot less attention than the football match of the previous week, but the passion and the nerves are the same. For the players, this is their biggest day, the day they have been preparing for all year.

The camogie roll of honour is a league table of the counties that have won the All-Ireland Senior Camogie Championship on the most occasions. Dublin heads the roll with twenty-six titles, followed by Cork with sixteen. But over the last twenty years, Kilkenny has been the most dominant team in the country, with twelve O'Duffy Cups to their credit. Of the many reasons for their success, arguably the most important, is the contribution of the Downey sisters. Twins Angela and Ann Downey have been with the team throughout the two decades of success, and Angela has captained the squad on four occasions. Angela debuted for the club in 1972, when she was only fifteen. Ann was a relative veteran of seventeen when she first wore the black and amber in Croke Park in 1974, but although she was only a substitute she claimed her first medal along with Angela.

Twenty years later Ann received the O'Duffy Cup in Croke Park as captain of Kilkenny, the twelfth title for the county and its star twins. As Ann stood there sodden in the rain after a very tough match, she departed from the normal decorum of the winner's speech, praising her sister as the greatest camogie player she had ever seen. Onlookers from all counties smiled.

Angela Downey is probably the best-known camogie player Ireland has ever produced. Even pundits who know nothing about camogie recognise the name Downey, Angela in particular. Her longevity, her skill, and her notoriety have combined to make her stand out.

A tenacious full forward, her goal-getting and attacking abilities for her county, club and college are legendary, earning her the unofficial title of the 'Christy Ring of camogie'. So too is her reputation for commitment and determination, her toughness on the pitch and her willingness always to carry on.

In 1993 Kilkenny lost to Cork in the semifinal of the All-Ireland Camogie Championship. The loss hurt Angela physically and emotionally, and she swore that her career was at an end. Officially she retired from the game, but twelve months later she was back in Croke Park, looking up wet and sweaty from the bottom of the Ard Chomhairle stand and watching as her sister Ann raised the O'Duffy Cup for the twelfth time. The thirty-seven-year-old twins had defied the sceptics to come back again, putting in stunning performances to bring the trophy back to Kilkenny. Angela scored two goals and two points of her team's tally, and after the match, her lips blue with the cold, she received the RTE award for 'Woman of the Match'. Not bad for someone who had retired the year before.

What made her return?

Ann exercised a little emotional blackmail, certainly. But it was also a love for the game. When Kilkenny lost to Cork in 1993, Angela was very upset. Some of the younger players were able to put the Cork loss behind them almost immediately, but not Angela. It simmered within her, and the following spring Ann had to use emotional pressure to entice her sister back. Ann had a co-conspirator in Angela's daughter Katie, not that the three-year-old was aware of her role.

Auntie Ann would tell Angela that Katie would be out on the pitch on finals day, with her mother looking down from the stands. The slagging hit home. Angela conceded and joined the panel in the spring. The Downeys were back in action.

The Downey twins are still behind Kathleen Mills and Una O'Connor of Dublin in individual All-Ireland medals, but they are certainly the best-known. Over the last two decades there is no doubt that Angela has been the most

Above: Angela Downey relaxing.

outstanding camogie player in the country – at least in the opinion of Brídin
Ní Mhaolagain, Uachtaráin Cumann Camógaíocht from 1991 to 1993. Brídin
knows Angela well, having competed against her in many an intervarsity
Ashbourne Cup match.

'Kathleen Mills and Una O'Connor were both outstanding in their own
day, but Angela is a totally different player to them. Kathleen Mills was
long and lanky whereas Angela reminded you of a Christy Ring
character. She is the same type of wiry striker of the ball, the way she
grabs the ball and turns from anywhere and takes a shot.'

Many players like to shoot, but Angela rarely misses, as she proved during her
debut in Croke Park when she was only fifteen. She proved it again twenty
years later, when despite the marking of the Wexford defence, she scored two
goals and two points from a minimum of possession. She had the ball perhaps
seven times in the match and scored on four occasions. Her combination of
speed, accuracy and strength set her apart from others. She is not afraid to go
in and get the score. She does not waste time and plays as if she has a built-in
radar.

As a full forward, Angela has often got the vital score that swung a match
in her team's direction, and her tenacious leadership abilities have added to

her strength in a side. She has trained with inter-county hurlers like Sean Stack, who were afraid to mark her. Eamon Cregan, manager of All-Ireland hurling champions Offaly, believes that both of the Downeys are of senior-level inter-county hurling standard, and better than the junior men.

'I know that she trained with UCD hurlers who were inter-county players like Sean Stack, and none of them would mark her; she was too good,' says Eamon Cregan. 'She's like Christy Ring in that you might keep her quiet for fifty minutes but then she'll wake up and bang, the damage is done,' he says.

Angela has also won five All-Ireland club championships with St Paul's of Kilkenny, losing only to Cork by a point in 1986. The following year St Paul's won the first of a historic three in a row, a feat which puts them on top of the league table for All-Ireland club championships with a total of eight titles. St Paul's disbanded in 1990, and Angela has since played with the appropriately named Lisdowney.

It was while playing for St Paul's in the All-Ireland club final of 1986 that Downey had what she considers to be one of her best performances. At half-time, Cork's Glen Rovers had scored four goals, and St Paul's had not yet breached the net. After the restart Downey lead a resurgence, scoring four of her side's five goals and a brace of points. In her efforts to breach the Rovers' defence, Downey received a head injury and had to leave the field.

St Paul's won the title by one point. Such determination to bear down on the opposition, despite the inherent dangers, is typical of Downey. Those who have not seen a camogie game live may think of it as a 'woman's sport', without much physical contact, but any close observer or player will tell you that there is plenty of close contact, much of it not accidental.

The 1994 final against Wexford was a particularly tough match, and both Downeys received considerable attention from the Wexford players. Kilkenny were also well able to give it back, and the action was not for the fainthearted. Players will tell you that camogie has developed into a far more physical game as teams and individuals have got much fitter and stronger. The stronger role played by men in the game in terms of training and coaching also means that more and more of the physical aspects of hurling are coming into the sport.

Club loyalties are also as strong for camogie players as for hurlers. Angela's first love at club level was and always will be St Paul's, despite her later career with Lisdowney, though to watch her play you would not think it. On the day before the 1993 All-Ireland camogie finals, Downey togged out for Lisdowney for her final appearance in a Kilmacud Crokes' Sevens tournament. At the age of thirty-six, she knew that there were questions from spectators about her presence on the pitch. But for Angela, even a minor game in the Dublin suburbs is highly competitive. Wherever she plays, she gives a hundred per cent. In a club match, if her team is winning by five or six goals, she still goes after another as hard as she can.

It infuriates her to see other camogie players do anything less.

In some ways it is unfortunate for Ann that she is her sister's twin. In another life, Ann would be the famous athlete, the camogie player that everybody talks about. It is only in the last five or six years that Ann has received the recognition she deserves. In Angela's opinion, Ann would always be doing the donkey work while Angela was getting the goals; and whoever gets the goals gets the mention in the paper. But Ann has a great read of the game. She plays in centre-field and can go back into centre-half position or play at full back or give a ball to someone in the half-forward line. And she is excellent at covering ground.

This last skill was particularly evident in the 1994 final. Despite her age, and the woman-to-woman marking, Ann played a terrific game. As well as feeding the forwards plenty of ball, she scored three points, accurately taken from frees. She was also the recipient of a number of swipes of the hurley, which she shook off to continue her role as centre-fielder and captain, urging on her young team-mates and acclaiming their scores. Ann's arms shot heavenward in the middle of the field when her sister slotted home Kilkenny's first goal of that match.

Since their days at boarding school in 1973, the twins have done everything together. (Though Ann has a record of achievement in other sports as well. She has represented Ireland at squash and has played hockey at a high standard.) After the first All-Ireland in 1974, they were always on the starting twelve. The twelve years the twin sisters have spent together on the Kilkenny camogie team have formed a particularly strong bond between them. After the victory in 1994, the pair embraced each other, clutching the cup between them and heading off to do the inevitable interviews for RTE. The emotions were in no way contrived – they were genuine expressions of two athletes with an enormous love and respect for each other.

The Downeys' skill and love for the game of camogie has both genetic and geographic roots. Growing up in Kilkenny, it was impossible to avoid the sport, and as their father, Shem, was a former senior county hurler, it was natural that the girls would take up a hurley and a sliothar. Though he was long finished playing by the time his daughters were growing up, it was natural for them to take up the sport.

The gate and the slaughterhouse roof served as the goals for the sisters at home, and tuition started at primary school with Matt Ruth's mother. It was at the Presentation College in Castlecomer, however, that the competitive camogie started for Angela. Her first memory of a competitive match was the junior county final when she was twelve.

Three years later Angela made her senior debut for Kilkenny, and the same year she ran onto the turf of Croke Park for her first All-Ireland final, the first of many. She remembers little of the day, just a blur of adrenalin, but she still scored 1-2, despite the fact that Kilkenny were beaten.

Both Downeys seem unaffected by success, despite their competitive edge. Angela is far from boastful of her achievements. Ann shows no bitterness about being in Angela's sporting shadow,

'I have honestly never felt that I live in Angela's shadow,' says Ann. 'As far as I am concerned her fame is totally deserved, she is simply a much better player than I am and probably the best camogie player ever. She just knows instinctively what to do with the ball whereas I'd probably pause and wonder what to do with it.'

That instinct to score is what Angela is all about. Opposing teams can often confine her to a few posessions of the ball, but she makes full use of those few snatches of the action. In the 1994 All-Ireland final, she had perhaps seven chances to score; she notched up two goals from hand passes and two floating points. The marking was good, but not good enough.

As soon as Angela got involved in camogie, it became a full part of her life, so much so that her mother moved her from Castlecomer to Saint Brigids of Callan, a boarding school where her mother thought she may concentrate on the academic side of school life. The opposite happened, though ultimately to her family's appreciation and delight. Angela played even more camogie at Callan than ever before, and it was from there that she took a foothold on the Kilkenny senior team.

After Callan came Maynooth for Angela and a degree in English and Geography. Maynooth in the seventies was even more male-dominated than it is now, and camogie was not a flourishing sport there when Angela arrived. That soon changed. Though Angela never won a national at Maynooth, the team did make it to two Ashbourne Cup finals. The hurlers took a great interest in the camogie players, and the team had its own pitch at the college.

The Ashbourne Intervarsity Cup has remained the only honour of the game to evade Angela, her one regret in her career. It is the oldest of all the camogie competitions, as it was established in 1915, so there is a certain sentimentality attached to winning the title. Intervarsity sport is always something of a lottery, as it depends on the availability of players; success is usually cyclical. In a small, male-dominated college like Maynooth, the odds against the team winning the cup were enormous, though on one freezing day in Casement Park, Belfast, Maynooth very nearly pulled off the unexpected.

The tournament was being hosted by Queen's University Belfast during a particularly cold winter. It is a wonder the final was played at all as the ground was frozen over so hard. Maynooth scored a memorable victory over the home team in the semifinal and then faced University College Galway in the final. Witnesses to the match remember it for Maynooth's remarkable style of play – or rather of two players in particular: Angela Downey and Chris Silke. Silke played at full back, so the tactic was for her to take all the puck-outs and deliver them straight down to Downey at full forward. Downey would calmly gather

Above: Angela Downey in action.

the sliothar with the entire UCG team bearing down on her, and more times than not score. Brídin Ní Mhaolagain remembers Angela and Chris carrying the Maynooth team. Galway only scraped a victory, winning by a single point. 'I'll never forget that match. It was an absolutely freezing cold day and Angela and Chris literally carried the Maynooth team. Chris would puck out the ball and Angela would bury it,' Brídin remembers.

Like her sister, Angela also tried her hand at other sports. At Presentation College, Angela was introduced to cross-country running, and most weekends she joined Kilkenny City Harriers, running in local and national competitions. She loved the sport and came home with nearly two medals every week. Running also helped her fitness, something that, despite her natural speed, she has never found easy to maintain, even to this day.

Weekly trips to the gym before starting teaching now supplement her efforts at keeping fit, though she admits she finds it harder all the time. And that is one of the reasons why Angela finally decided to retire from the sport of camogie at the age of thirty- seven, after winning her twelfth All-Ireland medal.

Unlike her previous retirement, this one looks permanent. After three knee operations, two on cartilage and another to remove a cyst, the sport has taken its toll over the twenty years. Another very important reason is her daughter. Angela was thirty-four when she gave birth to Katie, and since then camogie has had a rival in her life; a rival for which there is no competition. Angela and her husband, Ted, put off having children for many years because of the dominance of the sport in both their lives. (Though Ted had nothing to do with camogie until he met Angela, he now trains the minors.) Eight weeks after Katie's birth, Angela played for Kilkenny in the All-Ireland semifinal against Cork. That was 1990, and Kilkenny lost that semifinal. Angela came on as a substitute after the damage had been done.

'I shouldn't have really, I think it might have been a bit dangerous,' she admits. 'I felt as if all my insides were about to fall out and with hindsight I shouldn't have done it.'

After Katie's arrival, Angela could be seen on the sideline before a game, checking the child in her buggy and making sure she was warm enough before leaving her with Ted and taking to the field.

Angela's dedication continued, but it might not have been so. On October 23, 1988, a controversial incident kept her out of the game for six months, and could well have for good.

Downey was playing in an All-Ireland club semifinal for St Paul's against Killeagh of Cork. An incident between Angela and a Cork player, a bit of niggly play, occurred, though neither player was sent off. Angela misjudged a ball and fouled the opposing player, striking her on the ankle. The Cork player retaliated and hit Downey on the thigh. Angela fell to the ground. A free was awarded, and both players thought the incident had ended there, on the pitch. Neither realised what the referee's report had in store for them.

All such reports in the GAA remain secret, and only the resulting decision from the Camogie Central Council is made public. We will never know what was actually written, but whatever it was, Downey and her opponent were called upon to appear before the council. The council met in headquarters at Croke Park, and the players appeared as instructed, though separately. They were suspended for six months.

Downey was unhappy with the procedure. She is convinced to this day that the referee never saw the incident. Because she is a very well-known figure in camogie, Angela feels she was being used as an example of what not to do on the pitch. She felt hard done by, and nearly gave up the game. Around the same time, Meath footballer Gerry McEntee had struck a Cork player in the All-Ireland football final and was sent off. He received a suspension of two months. The disparity between punishments was galling to Downey.

As strong as her anger was, she did not give up the sport. She returned after the suspension and carried on for a further six years, until she was thirty-seven years of age and the mother of a two-year-old daughter. She maintains that the suspension was the most publicised incident of her career, to her intense annoyance. It received more attention than the seven All-Ireland titles in a row, her hundreds of goals and her resilience at playing at the age of thirty-seven, two years after the birth of her first child. RTE wanted her to come down to the studio in Waterford, the first time they had ever asked her to do that. She regards the incident and the response to it in the media as typical of the coverage camogie receives: token coverage until there is bad publicity, then saturation coverage. 'I got more publicity out of that than at any other time.'

The same reaction greeted the oft-quoted 'skirt incident'.

During an All-Ireland camogie final in which Kilkenny beat Cork, and in which Angela had scored a vital goal for Kilkenny, the overzealous marking of a Cork defender caused her to lose her skirt. Despite this mild distraction en route to the goal, Downey paid no heed, ran ahead, scored, and turning, raised her arms in triumph.

The front page of *The Irish Times* the following day featured a photograph of Downey in all her glory, having scored the goal with her boot, standing in her county shirt and underwear. Though the photo is framed at home in Ballyragget, it annoys Angela that she had to lose her clothes to get her photo on the front of *The Irish Times*. It was not the use of the photo that annoyed her, but that it takes an incident like that to get proper exposure for the camogie final.

Former President Brídin Ní Mhaolagain is similarly frustrated about camogie's stature as a sport and the amount of publicity it receives. She would love to see the day when there is a queue for tickets for the camogie All-Ireland final in Croke Park. But even though, at the end of 1991, there were 65,000 registered camogie players in Ireland, from under-twelves to over-thirties, an All-Ireland camogie final attracts a mere 6,000 people into Croke Park.

So what can be done?

Angela Downey's recommendation for bigger attendances is to schedule the camogie final on a day when there is another big match on; if they can organise hurling and football double bills after all, why not camogie as well.

'Exposure is what the game hasn't got, and needs,' says Downey. 'If I had my way in the morning I'd be playing the National League final, or even the All-Ireland itself, I'd be playing them as a curtain raiser to a National League hurling game. The GAA and the Camogie Association are two separate organisations. It's a "Catch 22" thing. You can't get away from them because we have no pitches so you have to go to them. Then Croke Park is only available on one or two days in the year for the "ladies day".

'As I said, my suggestion would be to have it as a curtain raiser to a big game and then at least you'd have people coming in or out and at

least they might stay and watch. A lot of people that do come and watch
the game, they say, "God, I didn't think they could play like that".'

In September 1993 the Cusack Stand was demolished as phase one in the
redevelopment of Croke Park, ceremoniously bid farewell to the Artane Boys
Band after the All-Ireland football final. A week later, with lumps gone from
the old stand and dust blowing around Croke Park, the All-Ireland camogie
final took place. Every year the president of the Camogie Association thanks
the GAA in her presentation speech for the loan of Croke Park. By being
separate to the GAA, an Cumann Camógaíochta is beholden to its bigger
brother.

As for relations between the camogie panel and Kilkenny's more famous
hurlers, getting physiotherapy and friendly advice is about as far as things go.
'We never trained with the hurlers, we wouldn't be let. We are lucky to get
into Nowlan Park when we want to get into it,' says Downey. And the early
exit of Kilkenny from the Leinster Championship in 1994 perfectly facilitated
the camogie panel. Nowlan Park was available to them all the way to the final.
'But seriously though, on a physical level, to train with the lads would be
madness. One jostle with them and you'd be killed. And the young lads — the
likes of D. J. (Carey) and P. J. (Delaney), they'd be out to prove a point like
"this one's not going to embarrass me now".'

Camogie's most famous daughter accepts, however, that the matter of
unequal treatment is not exclusive to her own sport and that it is a fact of life
that women's sport in general suffers from a lack of publicity and sponsorship.

'I don't think any women's sport will get the same as the men's,' says
Downey. 'I mean it's certainly improving, maybe in other sports more
than camogie, but there's still an awful long way to go. I often thought
that if I was fella, I'd have gone places, I'd have been in America so
many times or whatever. But you know, it's the same for someone with
ability born in the wrong county. When I look at someone like Sonia
O'Sullivan out there running for the big prize money, I say fair play to
you, because she could be gone in a few years and she's right to take the
opportunity while it's there.'

Yet the Kilkenny hurling team is very interested in the exploits of its female
counterparts, if not slightly bemused by the constricting rules of camogie —
the shortened pitch and small goals. Camogie is played on a sixty-metre pitch,
which is marked out within the larger hurling pitch with correspondingly
smaller goals. The length of the average puck-out in a game is ample proof
that the pitch is not adequate for the sport; to the average observer, it seems to
take away from the spectacle. Angela thinks they will go to full size eventually.

In the 1992/1993 league season, the Camogie Council experimented with a
fifteen-a-side format on the full pitch. It has been deemed a success and is
expected to be adopted for the championship season eventually. Unfortunately,
smaller counties cannot handle the larger dimensions, both in terms of pitch

size and team size. It is fine for strong counties like Kilkenny, Cork, Galway and Wexford, but much harder for the other counties to adjust.

Kilkenny hurler Adrian Ronan, who watched the Lisdowney team in their county club championship semifinal match, was astonished by the constricting rules under which the women had to play. He could not understand how the women managed to score, especially with smaller goalposts in front of the big ones.

But Angela Downey has managed to score for the last twenty-two years, in spite of all the obstacles. Although she has now retired from the inter-county game — or so she says.

Below: Angela and Ann Downey with the cup at Croke Park, 1994.

The twelve O'Duffy Cup All-Ireland senior camogie championship wins for Kilkenny and for Angela Downey:

1974 - Kilkenny 3-03; Cork 1-05, replay. (Kilkenny 3-08; Cork 4-05, draw)
1976 - Kilkenny 0-6; Dublin 1-02
1977 - Kilkenny 3-04, Wexford 1-03. (Captain Angela Downey)
1981 - Kilkenny 1-09; Cork 0-07, replay. (Kilkenny 3-09; Cork 3-09, draw)
1985 - Kilkenny 0-13; Dublin 1-05
1986 - Kilkenny 2-12; Dublin 2-03
1987 - Kilkenny 3-10; Cork 2-06. (Captain Angela Downey)
1988 - Kilkenny 4-11; Cork 3-08. (Captain Angela Downey)
1989 - Kilkenny 3-10; Cork 2-06
1990 - Kilkenny 1-14; Wexford 0-7
1991 - Kilkenny 3-08; Cork 0-10. (Captain Angela Downey)
1994 - Kilkenny 2-11; Wexford 0-8. (Captain Ann Downey)

National League Finals won by Kilkenny:

1978 - Kilkenny 2-04; Limerick 1-05
1980 - Kilkenny 3-08; Tipperary 1-03
1982 - Kilkenny 2-05; Cork 1-04
1985 - Kilkenny 4-07; Dublin 3-06
1987 - Kilkenny 4-08; Dublin 1-06
1988 - Kilkenny 3-10; Dublin 2-04
1989 - Kilkenny 6-07; Dublin 1-11
1990 - Kilkenny 1-10. Wexford 2-04
1993 - Kilkenny 4-07; Cork 1-13

Leading All-Ireland Senior Camogie Medal Holders:

Kathleen Mills, Dublin (15):	1942 - 1961
Una O'Connor, Dublin (13):	1953 - 1966
Angela Downey, Kilkenny (11)	1974 - 1991
Ann Downey, Kilkenny (11):	1974 - 1991
Gerry Hughes, Dublin (9):	1954 - 1963
Kay Rider, Dublin (9):	1955 - 1966
Bridie McGarry, Kilkenny (9)	1974 - 1991
Jo Dunne, Kilkenny (8):	1974 - 1991
Sophie Brack, Dublin (8):	1948 - 1956
Eileen Duffy, Dublin (8):	1957 - 1966
Kay Lyons, Dublin (8):	1957 - 1966
Eithne Leech, Dublin (8):	1959 - 1966
Marion McCarthy, Cork (8):	1970 - 1983

Cumann Camógaíochta na nGael: (1994)
Under-12: 12,015 players registered,
Age 12-17: 31,601players registered
Age 17-21: 9,071 players registered
Age 22-30: 9,164 players registered
Over 30:   3,193 players registered

All-Ireland Club finals in which Angela Downey played for St Paul's:

1974-75	St Paul's Kilkenny 3-03; Oranmore Galway 1-01
1976-77	St Paul's Kilkenny 6-03; Athenry Galway 1-03
1986	Glen Rovers Cork 4-11; St Paul's Kilkenny 5-07
1987	St Paul's Kilkenny 1-04, Glen Rovers Cork; 0-05
1988	St Paul's Kilkenny 4-05, St Mary's Glenamaddy 3-07
1989	St Paul's Kilkenny 6-10; Mullagh, Galway 4-02

Mary McKenna

Mary McKenna was born April 29, 1949, in Dublin. Attached to the Donabate Club, she has been the Irish Ladies Close champion eight times in twenty-one years, and runner-up for four years. She won the British ladies stroke play in 1979 and was voted Daks Woman Golfer of the Year in same year. With eight consecutive Curtis Cup appearances and membership on the Irish home international side from 1968 to 1991, she is one of Ireland's leading women athletes.

~

'I will play, and play at this standard, for as long as I feel I can.'

There is not a shadow of a doubt that Mary McKenna can still do it. She professes that as long as she can walk she will still play golf, and few question the sincerity of that statement. The bank official who first took up the game at the age of fourteen is still at the top of the women's game in Ireland, and it will be a while before she disappears from the scene. She loves the game, and she will keep playing as long as can.

Not long ago, it looked as if McKenna might bow out of the limelight. After twenty-four years of consecutive representation for Ireland in the home internationals, she was sensationally dropped from the team in 1992, without apparent explanation and, to many, without reason. She was shattered when it happened, particularly as she wasn't informed privately of the decision.

After twenty-four years of international service in the home internationals, the ILGU selection committee did not take Mary aside and inform her of their decision or their reasons. She was simply dropped after winning five inter-provincial matches that season.

McKenna is not bitter; but she is human and would have appreciated some courtesy.

'You've got to be realistic that with selection, ultimately it comes down to opinion. I was disappointed more in the way it was handled really, just the courtesy element of it. Also I was looking forward to my twenty-fifth in a row, and the thought of that was keeping me going, like any target. I had twenty-one and twenty-five was next so I suppose they put a spanner in the works by not picking me, but sure then you just put it behind you and carry on.'

(McKenna's feelings on the matter have not gone unnoticed, and it is now tradition that members of the previous years' team are informed privately whether or not they have made the cut again.)

The cut was a blow, but the following year McKenna was back and playing at the Hermitage in west county Dublin for Ireland in the home internationals.

She partnered twenty-year-old Aedeen Rogers for the three days, and her experience was proved on the final day, when she came back in her singles from two holes down to halve the match with England. Yet it was not enough for the Irish team to beat England overall. It was not a great year for the Irish in the home internationals, but Mary McKenna has seen it go better. The best-remembered was the win at Cruden Bay for Ireland in 1980, when Ireland won the triple crown though Mary is the first to insist that all caps are special. For her, playing for Ireland means as much now as it did when she was first capped.

Her captain at Hermitage in September 1993 was Susan Gorman.

'There's no doubt that Mary is missed if she isn't on any team. Her performance today in coming back like that is typical of her. On the 16th she holed a putt which showed huge character, then she got a fabulous three on the seventeenth and a birdie on the eighteenth.

'Mary really is the most recognisable of all the players. More men for example would know her better than plenty of the top men players.

'I don't know why Mary McKenna would even countenance retirement yet. Some thought that maybe last year was the time but she has proved them wrong. I, for one, will always be glad to have Mary around.'

Such notoriety is a long way from the days when the fourteen-year-old accompanied her mother to Donabate in 1963. Her mother's handicap was a beginner's 36, and as she played, the tall teenager took a shine to whacking the ball down the fairway. The following year she joined as a junior, and it soon became apparent that young Mary had not only a natural swing, but one of immense power, which was to propel her to the forefront of the women's game in Ireland. Within six years, Mrs McKenna's handicap was down to 24, while young Mary had won the Irish Women's Close Handicap at Ballybunion with a handicap of zero. Not bad for a relative novice.

After only two years at Donabate, McKenna had won the three major women's trophies at the club: the President's Prize, the Men's Captain's Prize for Women, and the Lady Captain's Prize. She also played basketball at school in Loreto Convent, North Great Georges Street, and was naturally sporty. Despite the fact that golf is essentially a solo sport, McKenna enthusiastically endorses the idea of playing a team game and always advises golfers to continue playing a team game. As golf is very self-centered, she argues it is healthy to withdraw and be a part of a team.

Anyone who plays golf knows how obsessive a player can become about the sport. The term 'golf widow' is not just a cliché, and although the single Mary has not left a widower at home, she is all too aware of how the game can preoccupy a person. In sports like tennis, a player generally plays against someone around the same level as herself. Golf allows players to compete with opponents at a much higher level.

Mary McKenna proved early on in life that she was well able to get the better of golf ball and most opponents. At 5ft 10ins she has never had a problem with power. Nowadays, however, plenty of players can hit it far. Equipment has improved as has the speed of the balls, like tennis. But skill and mental toughness are still what success is all about.

Luckily for McKenna, her strength and skill has been matched by a calm temperament which has served her well in fraught moments. She doesn't panic easily or often, but if she does, it's with very good reason.

When McKenna burst onto the scene in the sixties, only other women golfers were panicking. At the age of nineteen she made her first home international team, and by 1969 she became Irish champion for the first time at Ballybunion. Edmund Van Esbeck of *The Irish Times*, wrote this about her performance:

> 'A tranquil blue sky, warm sunshine and at the end of a perfect day, a new champion crowned. This was the setting that provided a fitting finale to a week of intense competition at Ballybunion, when twenty-year-old Mary McKenna swept away the frustration of defeat in last year's decider by capturing the Irish Women's Close Championship, with a 3 and 2 win over Mrs Catherine Hickey (Milltown). That it has taken Ms McKenna just 12 months in which to crash the barrier that divides the agonising feeling of getting one hand on the Cup only to have it snatched from her grasp, to the more ecstatic notion of placing it on her sideboard, is a striking tribute to the way she has learned her lesson and worked hard to achieve her objective. And Irish women's golf appears to have in her a player that has the potential to go on to greater things.'

How right he was. That was the first of eight Irish titles for McKenna in an era which, it could be said, was tinged with gold for women's golf in Ireland. Today, the game does not have as high a profile as it did in the past. The results just aren't there. In the seventies and the first part of the eighties, Ireland won two European titles, the home international, two British individual titles, three British stroke play champions and players getting regularly chosen for the Curtis Cup.

Equality for women may not have been high on the agenda back then, but McKenna was lucky in that the big banking groups in Ireland regarded sport very highly on a C.V. She was taken on by Bank of Ireland in 1968, and twenty-six years later, was still able to combine her job with her golf. She always gets leave for representative matches, whether interpros or internationals, and on her holidays she plays the scratch cups and other tournaments. In 1995, she finally took a year's leave of absence to concentrate on international competition. In the seventies and eighties, quite a few of the women golfers of the time were employed by the banks. McKenna, Rhona Brennan, Eileen Rose and Lyn Sweeney all worked with Bank of Ireland. The Wickham sisters and Sheena O'Brien-Kenney worked with Allied Irish Banks, and Claire Nesbitt was with the Ulster Bank. All in all, the bankers were quite a crop of international women golfers.

Today, more and more people are seeking work in their sport, or simply going pro, particularly in golf. More and more women are being taken on by clubs as apprentices and assistant professionals, and the discrimination issue is irrelevant. It is quite common to have a female assistant pro.

One such example is Aedeen Rogers, with whom Mary played doubles at the 1993 home international at Hermitage. In 1994 the twenty-year-old Rogers turned professional and was taken on by Portmarnock Golf Club in Dublin, an establishment known for an attitude that 'we don't discriminate against women because we don't have any women members'. Aedeen now represents Ireland all over Europe as a golf professional. Twenty years ago there weren't the opportunities for women in golf that there are now. Gillian Burrell was a pioneer for women in Irish golf. She now runs the driving range at Greystones. Now more and more women are going down that road.

Yet few Irish women think of going out on the pro tour. Mary McKenna certainly had the ability to do so, but at the time it was not really feasible, again for financial reasons. In the 1970s, there wasn't really a tour as such, and financially it wouldn't have been worth her while. Now there is a lot more money in the game, but the standard is very high.

In the area of discrimination in golf, McKenna admits that there is a long way to go.

'The real issue is time at the weekends, when everyone wants to play. Because of the numbers of members in clubs wanting time on the course, the minorities suffer and they are the women and juniors. Mind you I know of some cases where the junior boys get greater priority than women.'

If anybody has helped the lot of golfing women in Ireland, the successful Irish women's teams, of which Mary McKenna was a member, certainly have. Two European Championships and a Home International triple crown, all achieved in four years, are results that only come along occasionally.

In 1979 the Hermitage played host to the Women's European Golf Championships, which fourteen countries contested. The Irish team was Susan Gorman, Claire Nesbitt, Maureen Madill, Rhone Heggarty, Mary Gorry and Mary McKenna, with Moira O'Donnell as non-playing captain. It was the first time that the championships had been held in Ireland, itself a great honour for the country. The Hermitage is set around the lush and beautiful Liffey valley just east of Lucan. In a glorious setting huge crowds gathered to cheer the Irish women on once it became apparent that an upset was on the cards.

After thirty-six holes qualifying, Ireland lay in fourth position out of the best eight. They defeated Sweden four and a half to two and a half in the first round of the playoffs, following up with a four-match win over France in the semifinal. Now it was the final on home turf against Germany with an enthusiastic partisan crowd following every hole. A six-one victory made Irish golfing history. The scene was captured magnificently by

Caroline Walsh of *The Irish Times*:

'All day the estimated crowd of 4,000 trudged across the fairways and the rough and had perched their shooting sticks on the edges of bunkers to follow the Irish team's progress and when victory came shortly before eight o'clock, everyone was ecstatic.

'President Hillary, a keen golfer, who followed the girls' progress carefully, congratulated them all and reported that he had seen a great day's golf and was "absolutely thrilled" with the Irish victory. Within minutes the Garda Band, conducted by Sergeant John King, were responding to the occasion from under the sycamores with renditions of "Hallelujiah", "The Rivers of Babylon", and finally the National Anthem. At this point, and with some sense of decency, the sun suddenly graced the occasion with one great burst.

'Heinz Beimer, the non-playing captain of the German team and the only man among the eighty-four contestants, had virtually conceded defeat earlier in the evening when he said that the Irish team had saved him from having to shave all his hair off. The captain was referring to his promise made at an earlier stage of the event that he would cut off all his locks if his girls carried off the trophy.'

Below: Mary McKenna with the Hermitage Ladies Scratch cup

The win was a tremendous boost to golf in general. It was a joyous occasion, a great achievement with fantastic team spirit. It was the first time that Ireland had won anything in seventy-one years, and they did it on home soil. Only two years later, the Irish women were in storming form again, this time on the away links of Cruden Bay for the Home Internationals. On this occasion, Elaine Bradshaw was the non-playing captain, and she was optimistic about her team's chances. Bradshaw, McKenna, Nesbitt, Madill, Gorry and Gorman were joined by Claire Hourihane, and they were determined to keep their ambition focussed after narrowly losing out to Wales in the final of the previous year.

A first-day double loss to England in the foursomes was more than compensated by wins in the singles for McKenna, Hourihane and Gorman. Madill and Gorry halved their matches and Ireland had the victory by five-two. Scotland were beaten comprehensively on day two by six and a half to two and a half, and singles victories by McKenna, Nesbitt and Madill went a long way to securing the tie.

The final day was against Wales, and Ireland lead by two and a half to one and a half at lunchtime. Nesbitt won her singles and McKenna followed. A six and four win over Audrey Biggs inspired Maureen Madill to an eight and seven victory over Vicki Thomas. By now the end for Wales was near, and Gorry and Gorman followed with more singles victories. The result was Ireland eight and a half, Wales one and a half and the triple crown was theirs.

Two years later, Maureen Madill and Mary McKenna survived from the victorious Hermitage team to take on the might of Europe again at the appropriate battle ground of Waterloo, just outside Brussels. This was a European Championship that the Irish women were determined to capture against the odds, away from home.

McKenna and Madill joined with Claire Hourihane, Eavan Higgins, and Carol and Philomena Wyckham under the non-playing captaincy of Ann Heskin, who was assisted by Gerry Costelloe. Hourihane started the challenge in dramatic fashion by smashing the Royal Waterloo women's course record with a four-under-par 69. On a course which is made extra difficult by the preponderence of trees, Hourihane gave Ireland a flying start, and they duly qualified for the top flight, where they met Scotland. It was down to twenty-four-year-old Eavan Lynch to claim the limelight for Ireland with a win over Pamela Wright. A dramatic twenty-yard chip for a birdie three was followed by a missed putt from Wright, and Ireland were in the semifinals.

Sweden were the opponents and met their demise in muted fashion. It was now the final, against Ireland's greatest sporting rival, England.

Hourihane and Phil Wyckham beat their English opponents in the first foursomes. Mary McKenna and Eavan Higgins were then in a spot of trouble with three holes remaining and Ireland two down to the English. McKenna, the veteran of the Hermitage, kept her head on the sixteenth hole to pot a twelve-foot birdie. Her partner, Eavan Higgins, snatched a birdie on the seventeenth and halved the eighteenth. It was now a playoff, and a twenty-five-foot putt for a birdie by McKenna gave the Irish a two-nil lead and a huge advantage going into the singles.

Claire Hourihane prompted the Irish contingent into premature celebrations with a win over the reigning British champion, Mrs Thornhill, and Mary McKenna was next. A two and one win over Linda Bayman gave Ireland the necessary second victory to secure the trophy. Another win by Maureen Madill added the icing to the cake, along with a half by Eavan Higgins, and Carol Wyckham had no need to feel disappointed with her loss. Ireland were victorious at Waterloo.

It is a victory which Mary McKenna remembers with great affection.

'The first win at Hermitage was great, but in terms of excitement and achievement I think it was the second one for me which was more memorable. Hermitage was a shock win, because we had never won anything before and we were on home turf and all that. The following year was the first time to win the Home Internationals and that was very special. But Brussels was away from home, and we beat all of their rivals, Scotland and then England in the final. Now that was sweet. There were some fabulous matches and we proved that the first one wasn't a fluke.'

Another special international honour is to make the Curtis Cup team of British and Irish players. Mary McKenna has been selected for the Curtis Cup on no less than nine occasions, and she still does not rule out the possibility of reaching the magic ten. Many players regard being picked for the Curtis Cup team or for the male equivalent, the Walker or Ryder, as being one of the highest honours in the game.

The Curtis Cup is Britain and Ireland against the might of the US. In 1986 the venue was Prairie Dunes. The Britain and Ireland team, of which McKenna was a member, beat the US thirteen-five — the first time the Americans had ever been beaten on their home soil by either a Ryder, Walker or Curtis Cup team. McKenna was accompanied by both Lillian Behan and Claire Hourihane on the team. In all, Mary McKenna has played thirty Curtis Cup matches, won ten, halved four and lost sixteen. In comparison, the second most successful Irish woman to play in the Curtis Cup is Philomena Garvey, who between the years of 1948 and 1960 played eleven, won two, halved one and lost eight.

Having played in so many tournaments and on so many teams, McKenna has met hundreds of golfers. A few stand out. She considers her greatest influence Belle Robertson of Scotland. Mary played with her in her teens, and she was a person to look up to. She was very encouraging about Mary's golf and a great friend also, especially when she made the Curtis team and was the youngest player on it. Among Irish players, Ita Butler had a tremendous influence and was very encouraging, and Maureen Madill was perhaps the closest of many close friends in the game.

In 1995 Mary finally succumbed to temptation by taking a sabbatical from the Bank of Ireland. She divided her time between Ireland, the UK and Canada, doing what comes naturally — playing golf. She is regarded by most as one of the most outstanding women golfers that Ireland has ever produced. As she admits herself, her consistency over the years stands as testimony to that, although she would also single out Philomena Garvey as a great, though in a different era.

The McKenna era, however, has not yet ended.

Left: Eyeing up the putt.
Below: In the swing.

Ann-Marie Crowley-O'Brien

A nn-Marie O'Brien-Crowley has been involved in the equine world since she was a young girl in Pilltown, county Kilkenny. She learnt the trade through her father and was a champion pony jockey before she turned her hand to training with her husband Aidan O'Brien. The young couple have now built their own stables, have two yards and are among the most successful training operations ever to be established in Ireland. Ann-Marie and Aidan have one child, Joseph, and over one hundred horses in their care at their Owning stables.

~

The lush landscape of south county Kilkenny is unmistakeably horse country. *The Racing Post* sits alongside *The Kilkenny People* in local newsagents, and grazing horses are a common sight.

Just southeast of the Suir Valley lies the village of Owning. Drive through the small enclave and up the hill, and just as you begin to think you have taken the wrong turn, the wide grey gates of Caraiganog Stables appear on the steep incline of the slope. Continuing up the winding drive, a new grey building stretches out, complete with clock tower in the style of the RDS. These are the stables built by Ann-Marie and Aidan.

Ann-Marie Crowley-O'Brien welcomes you into the kitchen and introduces you to her son Joseph, who is playing in his pen situated in the middle of the floor. She smiles an unaffected welcome and enquires as to whether you found the stables all right. Outside, Aidan and the stable lads are riding out the horses over the tracks on the hillside, overlooking in the mist the flat Suir Valley below.

Ann-Marie Crowley-O'Brien is a mother, horse trainer, ex-jockey and ex-model. Model? Surely a stroll along the catwalk is out of place with this life of domestic and equine bliss. It may be now, but a few years ago the occasional stint on the ramp helped Ann-Marie pay her way through college and subsidised her racing and early training career.

Such a background has advantages and drawbacks. As soon as it became known to the media that an ex-model was training horses *and* winning, Ann-Marie was inundated with requests for interviews, all of which began with undisguised curiosity about her modelling. Sometimes it infuriates Ann-Marie that this is one of her most famous attributes. The South-East modelling agency of Anne Burke, however, knew her as a very dependable and a very good all-rounder. 'She was very good on the ramp, and she has a very photogenic face, so she could do any kind of modelling work,' says Anne.

To her credit, Ann-Marie Crowley-O'Brien has never tried to milk her past career, nor her gender, for any publicity. She has traditionally shunned the limelight and has been a very reluctant interviewee, in many cases flatly refusing requests from newspapers. She also instructed her former employers in the model agency not to release any of their publicity photos of her.

These actions are not borne of arrogance but from a shyness and a priority to keep her life private. She loves her life with Aidan, Joseph and the horses, and does not lose any sleep over what others think of her.

Which brings us back to the horses, and the reason why the name Ann-Marie Crowley-O'Brien attracted any publicity in the first place. In the latter half of 1992 the name Ann-Marie Crowley-O'Brien became a regular as the winning trainer on flat races. In two months she notched up twenty winners, and people sat up and took notice. She certainly has the lineage. Her father, Joe Crowley, encouraged his six daughters to ride from an early age, and as the youngest, Ann-Marie, set the pace on the family farm. 'When you've been brought up with horses, you can't think of doing anything else,' she says.

Ponies were the mounts when they were children, and she rode her first when she was around five years of age. This pattern continued during her teens as she extended her knowledge of the whole horse industry, down to shoeing the horses on the farm. 'We didn't have a farrier, so myself and Dad would do the shoeing,' she says.

Her eighteenth birthday was a landmark, not just as the end of her childhood but because she made a choice about the direction her life would take. For her birthday, her parents offered her a choice, a party or a horse. She chose the horse, a filly called Lunalae on which she won two races.

Pony-riding had not been just a hobby or playtime on the farm. It is the nursery school of all jockeys, and most young riders who show some talent on the smaller mounts go on to try their hands as amateur jockeys. 'I registered as a jockey when I was seventeen and had twenty-four winners in all,' she says.

Before she had been riding for two years, she was ladies champion jockey. There were only a few women racing at that stage, including Caroline Hutchinson, Sandra McCarthy, Susan Finn and a Swedish girl named Lulu, and Ann-Marie beat them all at some stage.

Ann-Marie is taller than the average jockey, so her success may seem a little surprising. However, at that early stage a jockey's weight does not make an awful lot of difference. When it came down to it, it was skill which was the significant factor. It is in the professional ranks that weight really matters.

The life of a professional jockey was not for her, however. Any professional jockey, male or female, has to have the backing of a stable to get regular rides. In most cases you also have to be able to get work in that stable or another for when you are not racing. Income must be sustained, and if you are not winning, or indeed racing regularly enough, you will not earn. 'I was lucky in that I had my father to give me rides,' she says. 'It's very hard for anyone to build up the experience. It's like having a portfolio of races and you really do need to have a stable behind you.'

Ann-Marie also knows only too well the physical back-up that's needed on the circuit and the fact that facilities for women jockeys, while improved greatly in recent years, are still light years behind those of their male couterparts. Any improvements at all are due to efforts of people like Ann-Marie herself and Sandra McCarthy. It was they who tired of changing in the ambulance room or in the ladies' toilets and decided to do something for themselves and their colleagues.

They decided to do something about conditions in 1990. Ann-Marie and her fellow-jockey Sandra McCarthy took matters into their own hands and formed the Lady Riders Association, which is still in existence, though not as strong as it was in the early years.

'It was set up primarily to get more ladies' races, and it achieved that all right. Like I said I was in the lucky position of being able to get rides from my Dad's horses and so was Sandra, but many aren't and we felt that they needed some self promotion as a group,' says Ann-Marie.

'One of the main achievements in that sense was the establishment of a sponsor for a series of races, and Dunnes Stores came up with the goods on that, and they were still going up until recently anyway.'

The association also did its best to publicise the bad facilities for women jockeys at race courses. Punchestown and Gowran Park have apparently spruced up their operations considerably, and they are now two of the best in the country for women's facilities.

'The association made people recognise that there are lady riders on the courses who also need facilities and sponsorship. What the association achieved was that it made a lot of people on the courses pull up their socks and provide facilities, and there was a great improvement.'

Although Ann-Marie was involved in the initial stages of the association, she has since become detached from their activities, which is hardly surprising since she turned to training horses herself and thence to rearing her son. She would not balk at the idea of becoming involved in the administration of the equine world at a later stage — perhaps on the National Racing Authority.

Yet she knows she could never take a job like that lightly; it would demand her full-time attention.

While supporting the idea of women getting more involved in such matters and improving their lot, Ann-Marie does not agree with the tokenism in such matters.

'I read in the paper that the Minister was going to recruit some women as representatives on the board, like choosing women because they are women rather than because they are qualified for the job. There's no point in doing that, doing the politically correct thing because you are trying to be diplomatic. That doesn't do anybody any good.'

Her career as a trainer also began at an early age. Her father started training originally and sold on a number of 'bumpers' for the first year or two. (A bumper is a national hunt horse which starts off running flat races.) The next step was to take out a trainer's license. Her father didn't want to take the license out, so Ann-Marie did, and by the time she was twenty she was training ten or eleven horses.

'To get the license you go through one of those "Catch 22" situations, where you have to have a number of horses in training and then be recommended by two trainers as well to The Turf Club. You simply ask people, apply, and then either get accepted or rejected,' she says.

In Ann-Marie's case rejection was never really in the picture and she was given the green light to carry on.

'Back then was before we got big, and it was so much easier. I was about twenty, nearly twenty-one at the time and we had ten or eleven horses. It only took myself, my father and a few of the lads to manage. I wish it was that easy now.'

Her then boyfriend Aidan O'Brien started helping out also, and within a year it had become the complete family business, with Mr and Mrs A. O'Brien running the show. Ann-Marie originally met Aidan on the racecourse, and he too came from a strong horsey family. His father trained point to pointers and showjumpers at their farm in Clonroach County Wexford. Their marriage in 1991 coincided with their starting to train a few winners, and the business has grown since then. The O'Briens started building the Carraiganog stables in 1993, and by May 1994 they had over seventy horses in the yard.

The doubling up of numbers makes the job much more difficult. They had to split the horses between two yards, one of which is beyond the gallop, at a distance that can be quite awkward. The gallops of Carraiganog loop up over the side of the hill to the east, then turn back south and over the edge of the brow of the hill to where the long straight run stretches out and the horses can open their lungs and test their limbs. The run is crunchy underfoot, with brown wood filings and old straw, and there is a rythmic thudding as a bunch of lads and their mounts canter by, rugs on the backs of the horses, their light brown helmets like premature conkers. They shout hellos in the mist as they go by, all adrenalin and chestnut-brown sinews. It looks great, and Ann-Marie clearly misses the buzz of the early morning runs.

A few years earlier, she would start the riding out at 7:00 am, continue until lunchtime, work out the horses in their boxes, and then either ride out some more in the afternoon or go to a race meeting. Now her younger sisters Francis and Angela help out with a lot of the riding out, and sibling Breda works in the stables, making it truly a family enterprise.

Ann-Marie misses the racing, but there is nothing to compare with training. The training took over and became her full-time occupation and preoccupation — it is more than just fun. Anybody who has ridden and trained knows the buzz of training a winner. It seems to be the same sort of satisfaction a former footballer swears he feels if he succeeds in management. Ann-Marie agrees wholeheartedly with this theory.

Left: Ann-Marie and her son, Joseph.
Below: Aidan with Joseph and the winning 'Glounnthaune Garden' at Leopardstown, 1994.

'Absolutely, you get more satisfaction as a trainer than a rider. It's an achievement to get it to the track in the first place, because they are exposed to so many illnesses and bugs in the yard, and then, on the course itself it's even worse. If they run at all it's great and if they win it's terrific. It makes everything worthwhile.'

It seems that her days of enjoyment as a trainer have not been too rare on the racing calendar. Turf Club records show that Ann-Marie O'Brien had six National Hunt winners in the 1990/91 season, eighteen the following year, and a whopping fifty-three in the 1992/93 season, making her the leading National Hunt trainer for that year — not bad for a twenty-three-year-old. On the flat, she trained ten winners in 1991, seven in 1992 and two in 1993. Her most treasured moment was Beirut winning a £50,000 race at Punchestown in 1993.

Ann-Marie Crowley-O'Brien gave up her training license in June 1993, after she became pregnant with her son, Joseph. Aidan then took over the name on the license and the success has continued at Carraiganog. Since transferring the license to Aidan's name, Ann-Marie has not been as involved in the day-to-day physical activity, but there has been more than enough paperwork to keep her going.

Aidan O'Brien's success is now legendary in Ireland, but Ann-Marie is in no way jealous. It is, after all, a family business, and these days her name may not be on the license, but somebody has to manage the commercial end of things. Ann-Marie is doing this quietly and competently.

While Joseph is still young, she will maintain that role, but not for long. The buzz of having your own winner come into the enclosure is still lurking there, only waiting to be rekindled.

Michelle Smith

Michelle Smith was born in 1970. At age eighteen she participated in the 1988 Olympic Games in Seoul, swimming the 400 metres individual medley and placing seventeenth. From 1989 to 1992 she was a scholarship student at the University of Houston, Texas. At the World Championships in Perth in 1991 she placed tenth in the 400 metres individual medley and earned a twenty-first place finish in the same event in the Barcelona Olympics the following year in spite of back problems. Since then she has had a consistent record of international success, including several Irish records, a world ranking of fifth in 1994 and silver and gold medals in the European Cahmpionships in 1995.

~

'It's just you, your time and the wall.'

Michelle Smith will never forget September 11, 1994. Not only did she win her heat in the 200 metres butterfly in the World Championships, but she also finished fifth in the final, the highest that an Irish swimmer has ever placed in a world championship. It also happened to be the day that Erik lost the ring.

Erik de Bruin, Michelle's Dutch boyfriend, watched her heat from the camera podium behind the starting blocks. Pretending to be a TV technician, he got an excellent vantage from where to watch Michelle. Every time she took a tumble turn below him, he called out, 'Keep your concentration'. All the hours of coaching, training and videoing were now at an end, and he stood helpless, willing Michelle through the water. Tied to his shorts were hotel keys and the ring, the engagement ring he had given Michelle a few short months after they had met at the Barcelona Olympics.

Two hours later, Michelle Smith knew that her win in her heat had not only broken the Irish record but guaranteed her a place in that evening's final, the first time she had ever qualified for a World Championships 'A' final. Michelle and Erik returned to their hotel, exhilarated at the news. Erik untied the key from his shorts and, unknown to them at the time, the ring fell onto the floor. A little while later Michelle asked him for the ring so she could wear it for the few hours before her swim in the final. He looked at her. The ring was gone. 'I was probably the happiest I had ever been for one minute and then I was devastated,' remembers Michelle. As Erik watched her face fall, he knew he had to intercede. There was a race that evening after all. 'Don't worry about the ring, we'll get another one, concentrate on the race,' he declared.

But putting its loss behind her, she went through her relaxation motions before the final. She lunched on pasta, and then rested, falling deeply asleep, a knack she has always had. (Some athletes find it difficult to switch off before a race.) After her sleep, Michelle put on her discman and concentrated on the race ahead. 'Simply the Best' by Tina Turner was her choice, and it was no accident. Before a race, she always plays something upbeat to get the adrenalin going. 'It kind of psyches you for the effort ahead.'

The final was on at six o'clock, and as her parents tried to locate a television with Eurosport back in Dublin, Michelle prepared for her biggest moment. The butterfly had never been considered her strongest event, but on her red-letter day she was swimming that very stroke. She decided not to think about the medals, but just to swim as fast as she could, and do the best race possible.

Swimming is very different from an athletics final. In a track race, tactics count for an enormous amount, and the runners are constantly watching for other runners making a move. In a pool, the swimmer concentrates on her own lane and the wall at the end. Even if she wants to, it is only possible to see those swimmers in immediately neighbouring lanes. So she must swim the distance at her own pace, touching the wall at the end of the distance and looking up to see what happened — 'It's just you, your time and the wall.'

In her heat on the morning of September 11, Michelle was in lane seven, at the edge of the line-up, and far away from the much fancied Americans in the middle lanes. (Traditionally, those expected to perform the best swim in the middle lanes, hence the oft-seen fan shape of swimmers in races.) Michelle made up her mind before the race that she would pay no heed to any other swimmer, even if she became aware that a few were breaking out ahead. She stuck to her pace and strengthened as she went on, finally touching the wall and looking up at the board to see where she had finished. 'I just saw "1. Smith - Ireland" and the time, and I realised I'd done it. Erik was shouting, and then we just had to wait to see if I'd made the final.'

Another difference between swimming and athletics is heat qualification. In running, the first few places in each heat and the fastest losers qualify for the final. In swimming, it is the fastest seven or eight overall who qualify for the 'A' final, and the next group in time make the 'B' final. A win in a heat does not guarantee qualification. An hour's wait told them what they needed to know: Michelle had the fourth fastest time overall and was in her first 'A' final.

The Irish woman was a rank outsider in the race, and she knew that she had nothing to lose. She went for it, and finished in fifth place, the highest ever placing by an Irish swimmer in a World Championships A final, and another Irish record. She took three seconds off the Irish record for the 200 metres butterfly between the two races.

Just over a month previously Michelle had to abandon her training after she was struck down by a kidney infection. She didn't think that she would make it to the championships in Rome, and her health was her priority. To come back to full training, and to finish in fifth place in the final of an event which was traditionally not her favourite, was an astonishing achievement.

What is even more startling, however, is the fact that Michelle Smith comes from a country which does not have even one full-size international Olympic-standard swimming facility; no fifty-metre pool.

'Restrict Christy O'Connor Jr or Ronan Rafferty to playing at home on a pitch and putt course and then ask them to go and try to do well in the US Masters. That would be about the size of it,' said Sean Gordon of the ASA, after Michelle finished fifth in the world.

Asking swimmers like Michelle to train in a pool which is less than the correct length is unfair. Swimming is not just about speed, but about timing, breathing and turning as well. When a swimmer is racing at twenty-five metre events, her turns become much more important because they are a much more substantial part of the race. She has to change her breathing and timing accordingly and learn to swim longer and stronger for the greater distance.

However, the building of a fifty-metre pool will not guarantee that Ireland will produce a World or Olympic Champion within years.

Also, those who believe a fifty-metre pool will bring top-class international events to Ireland should think again. The venue for the 1994 swimming World Championships in Rome had one fifty-metre pool, a diving pool, a water polo pool, two smaller pools, and a synchronised swimming pool. A temporary prefabricated pool was also built on site to facilitate practising. To host a major international championship, you really need two fifty-metre pools one to swim in and one to practise and warm down in.

For Ireland to consider itself a top sporting nation, it must act like one. Since the Barcelona Olympics in 1992, Michelle Smith has been lucky enough to be able to get time in a Dutch fifty-metre pool; in essence this Irish athlete has effectively been sponsored by the Dutch Olympic Council. She and Erik stay in Dordrecht in Holland, near Rotterdam and close to Erik's family. There are three or four fifty-metre pools within half an hour of their apartment, and the Dutch Olympic Council recommended a coach for Michelle. He is based in one of the pools and also coaches a Dutch girl. They give Michelle a lane of her own to train in, and there is a gym nearby where Erik helps her work out.

In 1994 the Dutch Olympic Council went a step further and offered full-time training, a car and a Dutch passport if Michelle would change her allegiance. Flattered by the offer, the Dublin woman refused this very favourable deal. The first Irish woman to carry the tricolour in the Olympic Games was not going to give up her birthright.

The influence of Erik de Bruin on Michelle Smith is considerable. The couple met at the Barcelona Olympics after another Irish athlete, Perri Williams, asked Michelle along to meet her Dutch boyfriend. Erik arrived with him, and that was that. They had both been to the Seoul Olympics but never met. After Barcelona, Erik returned with Michelle to Dublin, and the pair have been virtually inseparable since, dividing their time between Holland and Ireland and concentrating on Michelle's training while Erik has been nursing an injury. After Barcelona, Erik looked at her swimming and schedule and said that European athletes used to train that way fifteen years ago. Now methods had improved. She had never done sprint work before or worked with weights, so Erik devised a programme to introduce those elements to her training.

Erik reasoned that if she could reduce her sprint times she could reduce her overall times by speeding up the end of the long-distance race. As they tried it out, it became obvious that the new methods worked. They also looked at Michelle's diet and increased her carbohydrate intake. Now she eats a lot of potatoes and pasta, but she confesses that she does not like vegetables very much! Like Erik, she also takes courses of vitamins. (There is also room for certain luxuries like chocolate, and both Erik and Michelle allow themselves a few sinful morsels with a cup of coffee every evening.)

Michelle rises at 5:30 am and trains from 6:00 to 8:30. At 9:00 she has breakfast and then goes back to bed. A few hours later she works out in the gym and, then they both eat their main meal in the middle of the day. In the afternoon they look at her stroke work, and then she trains for another few hours. In the evening they relax. Rest is an important a part of her training.

Erik has also helped Michelle with her stroke work, looking at it on video and comparing with other top swimmers. They have spotted tendencies on video that need a slight adjustment.

'When you are swimming at world championship level, even the tiniest of changes or differences can mean an improvement in your time. It may seem a very small improvement, but it can make the difference between eighth and tenth in a race,' maintains Michelle.

The weight training has also showed its benefits. Michelle is quite small for a swimmer, and it was a joke for a long time when she was young that she wasn't big enough to have what it takes. Now the work on her upper arms in the local gym in Holland is proving beneficial.

Michelle freely admits that she swims better in the evening, but early-morning starts are part of a swimmer's lifestyle, from junior level with a local Irish club up to international standard. It was Brian Smith who drove his daughters to Tallaght and Kings Hospital for those early morning plunges, and it was he who first introduced his family to the sport. Michelle's father was keen that they be involved in a sport, and from a safety aspect he decided to bring them swimming. Michelle was only about four or five, and she used to pester him to bring her, so she began to swim more and more.

When Michelle was nine, her instructors in Tallaght noticed that the small girl was showing more talent than was usual at that age, and she was advised to go to Kings Hospital for more training. She was training with a few swimmers like Kevin Williamson and Catherine Bohan. She was only ten, and her fellow trainees were already competing internationally.

The ten-year-old had an unusually natural ability at the backstroke (most young swimmers favour the freestyle event), and at that young age she was

Above: Michelle Smith with her father, Brian.

doing up to five hours a week of early training. By the time she was twelve, her hours had increased to over ten, something that she now has some reservations about.

'I was a bit young, I think, to do that much. Nowadays coaches are being a bit more cautious about overtraining children. In Germany, for example, swimmers start the really rigorous training after they reach sixteen. If you start heavy training at ten, by the time you reach twenty you'll be sick of it.'

Every morning Brian waited for Michelle to wake him to drive her down to the pool, wrapped in blankets. There was tremendous support, but there was no question of pressure. If Michelle did not want to go training, Brian would not force her to do it.

At the age of ten, Michelle started competing and winning, despite her small size. Her coach, Derry O'Rourke, still wondered if she was too small to make it, but what Michelle lacked in strength she made up for in technique. She compensated for her smaller size by developing her style with a kick twice as strong as the girls she was racing against. Her will to win and her talent compensated for her lack of physical strength.

Michelle's sister Sarah also swam, but she enjoyed the social end of the life more than the hard work and the competition. When Sarah was preparing to do her Leaving Cert she decided to give up swimming. There were no pressures to continue. In the meantime Michelle was combining swimming and studying as best she could while attending school at Coláiste Killian in Clondalkin. Her teachers were very good and understood that she had to train and do competitions. Michelle was supposed to do her Leaving Cert in 1988, but she was away training in Canada and Florida in preparation for the Seoul Olympics. In the end, she sat her English paper and then flew to Florida for the pre-Olympic training camp. While other students thought of the matric, Michelle flew to Seoul to represent her country at the Olympic Games.

Seoul was her first Olympics, and even though she thoroughly enjoyed Barcelona as well, Seoul was special because she was eighteen and everything was so new. She finished in seventeenth place in the 400 metres individual medley and missed out on qualifying for the final by a tenth of a second. Her father was there, at the biggest competition of her life. There were five thousand people on either side of the pool, the biggest crowd she had swum in front of by far.

After Seoul, Michelle returned home and continued her training. Scholarship offers started coming in and the US beckoned. There wasn't an option of studying in Ireland on a sports scholarship, and even if UCD's scheme had been up and running at that stage, the lack of a swimming pool on the campus would have mitigated against it. After all offers were considered, and with six subjects in her Leaving under her belt, Michelle opted for the University of Houston, a time she looks back on now with mixed feelings.

'I think it benefited me at the beginning but not at the end. The training was very regimented, and you were reminded all the time that you were swimming for the university and that was it. There were a lot of other international swimmers there as well, and that was fun, but after a while, just competing against other universities in the US wasn't enough. Also the competitions were in twenty-five-metre pools, so while I was used to that, I also needed to get more experience in fifty-metre pools. And another thing, Texas was not the place to be for a woman who liked to think for herself.'

The American college swimming season finished in February, and as exams didn't take place until May, Michelle had to arrange to have the pool opened up so that she could train on her own for the three months. Such a lonely regime was not great for her morale, and she often thought she would have been better off back in Ireland.

Michelle did not graduate from her course in communications at Houston. She took a year off in 1992 to prepare for Barcelona, and apart from a brief return, she decided that her days there were over. (She would like to finish her degree in Ireland at some point in the future.)

Barcelona 1992 was Michelle's second experience of the Olympics, and although it was not the success that many hoped, it marked something of a turning point in her career. Since then she has got better and better. She had problems with her back that summer when two discs wore away. Three weeks before the Olympics she couldn't do tumble turns, but she was so stubborn she still competed. 'In retrospect, maybe I shouldn't have gone, but at the time if you had tried telling me that, then I wouldn't have listened to a word.'

Michelle finished in twenty-first place in the 400 metres individual medley with a time of 4.56, the exact time she had recorded in the World Championships in Perth the year before, and which had placed her tenth. Such are the vagaries of times and races.

Barcelona may not have been the career highlight that she wanted, but it did bring her a moment that she will cherish forever; carrying the Irish flag in the opening ceremony — 'The highlight of Barcelona and maybe of my life.'

A picture of Michelle marching with the flag adorns the family home in Dublin, but sadly nobody in Ireland saw it because at the moment Michelle walked into the stadium on Montjuic in Barcelona, the television cameras chose to switch their attention to a team lining up.

Since Barcelona and meeting Erik, Michelle has devoted her life to being a full-time athlete. In 1993 she was unlucky to miss out on the European Championships due to a bout of glandular fever, but that may have enabled her to surprise observers at the World Championships in Rome in 1994. As her training methods have become more sophisticated, her times have improved dramatically, surprising even herself. At twenty-four years of age, Michelle Smith finally started fulfilling her potential. In another country that might be considered late, but like many other Irish athletes she is a late developer.

Since Michelle gave up college and became a full-time swimmer, finance has become a much bigger consideration. She has always received Cospoir grants, and while they have not been huge she is reluctant to criticise them or the Olympic Council who omitted Michelle from their elite sportspersons' grants in 1994. Up to 1993 she received £1500 from Cospoir. In 1993 it went up to £3,000, and in 1994 she received £7,500 on their 'Oustanding Sportspersons' grant scheme. She didn't get an OCI elite grant in 1994 because they said that she hadn't proved herself in a fifty-metre pool. 'At the time, it was probably fair enough. I don't think there's any point in griping on about it because it's not as if I'd give up swimming without the money. I'll still do what I want to do,' she says.

Michelle is not afraid to be outspoken, and she has plenty to say when she feels that things are not going as she would like them to. She has had her ups and downs in her relationship with the Irish Amateur Swimming Association, and she feels that bureaucracy sometimes gets in the way of an individual's success. In 1993 she was not entered in some Grand Prix meets which would have netted her a considerable amount of money if she had succeeded in them.

In 1994, however, she joined the stable of Irish sporting stars with agents. Frank Quinn, the man who handled Sean Kelly's highly lucrative career, felt that Michelle Smith was worth taking on as a client, and he added her name to his books. Such a contact is probably the best way of approaching potential sponsors, and in the fickle world of sporting finance such back-ups are vital rather than just luxuries.

With sponsorship, agents want athletes with intelligence and personality, and Michelle has both.

'When you're a woman in sport you want to attract sponsors who deal in beauty and health-care products. Michelle is a successful Irish swimmer with a good personality, and contrary to the popular image of the sport, she has fabulous long hair, which is a sponsorship plus,' says her agent Frank Quinn (Colet hair products are one of her sponsors).

There are also her nails. The day after she swam in the World Championships final in Rome, a large colour photo appeared in *The Irish Times* sports section of Michelle swimming in her heat. Clearly visible is the green shamrock on her cap, and ten red varnished nails, plunging into the water. 'You wouldn't believe the amount of people who have commented on my nails,' she remarks.

But beauty products are not her only sponsorship resource. In 1994 TNT Express Couriers decided to back her, and they are now her main sponsor.

Michelle Smith's attitude to her sporting career is utterly professional, and she refuses to let circumstances stand in her way. For example, as regards the rise of Chinese women in international swimming, she was adamant that their success cannot put her off her goals. 'I can't think about them, because if I do I might as well just give up.'

In November 1994, after so many Chinese swimmers were tested positive for doping, she did wonder about what may have been possible in Rome. She finished in fifth place behind four other swimmers, including two Chinese. They all failed the controls because of the same substance, hydrotestosterone, which annoyed Michelle.

'When I finished fifth in the 200 metres in Rome that September, I was just so proud and pleased. I never thought of the fact that the Chinese girls had finished first and second. But now I'm beginning to think that Susan O'Neil, Matte Jacobsen and myself were robbed of our rightful rewards.'

Ironically, these revelations coincided with another tremendous achievement for Michelle Smith. On Sunday, December 11, she won the 100 metres backstroke in an international meet in Dordrecht in Holland, setting a new Irish record of 25.85. The win also put her at number one in the world rankings for the 100 metres butterfly. That was the first time that any Irish swimmer had been ranked at number one in the world for any stroke over any distance.

What about heroes? Perhaps surprisingly, Michelle singles out boxer

Above: *'It's just you, your time and the wall.'* Michelle Smith..

Wayne McCullough, someone for whom she has great admiration and someone else who carried the Irish flag in an Olympic Games.

Michelle Smith is happy to do her own thing, and her swimming performances continue to improve dramatically. Perhaps she is similiar to Wayne McCullough in that even though the 'Pocket Rocket' is not regarded as having a solid knockout punch, he wears his opposition down with his fitness and consistency. Michelle Smith may not have the big physique and strength of her opponents, but what she is lacking she makes up for in training and in technique.

In 1994, Irish swimming went through something of a rough time due to the publication of a story alleging sex abuse in the sport. As the investigations proceeded and the accusations flew, Michelle Smith did her bit for the sport in producing some of the best performances ever achieved by an Irish swimmer. Through the winter of 1994-95 she took no less than eleven World Cup medals in a season when the entire Irish squad won twelve! At the end of the World Cup season, she won the overall Grand Prix prize for the butterfly and a prize of $7,000. But 1995 was the best of all.

The swimmer from Rathcoole continued to improve her form in early 1995, with a series of great wins in the short course World Cup series. Holland was still the base with access to fifty-metre pools and better training methods, but it was perhaps because of this that a certain amount of innuendo floated between the lines of print back in Ireland.

The main reason for this was Michelle's relationship with, and coaching by, her Dutch boyfriend Erik de Bruin. A former Olympic silver medallist in the discus, de Bruin tested positive for a banned substance and was consequently debarred from international competition by the IAAF. The fact that he was Smith's swimming coach and that her times seemed to have radically improved lead to rumour, and plenty of it. It was a case of guilty by association.

Because of this, Smith was almost relieved when a knock on her door in April revealed drug testing officials from the Dutch Olympic Council. 'I was making dinner and was up to my elbows in salmon so I guess you could say that it was fairly unexpected all right,' she laughs. Salmon or not, the testers set to their task, taking samples A and B from the Irish swimmer. 'It went fine, I gave them the samples and as it was out of competition it was designed to catch me out if there was anything to find.'

The thing about a drug test is that you will only hear from the men in white coats again if you have tested positive. Negative testing means silence, so no news is good news. Two months later, Smith knew that she was 'in the clear' so to speak, and she spoke about the experience and the innuendo when she was next in Dublin.

> 'The first time I heard what people were saying I just got really angry, but then I realised that was stupid. I mean these are people who don't know the ins and outs of Erik's case and then they presume stuff about me. They must think I'm stupid, I mean you get tested all the time in competition, and now I've been tested outside of competition as well; I'm clean and that's that.'

Certainly it must be said, that if observers were to look for signs of steroid use in Michelle Smith's physical appearance, there is no indication of the tell-tale acne, nor bloated features. She is a small girl with strong upper body strength, a testimony she says to training and newly discovered gym routines.

On that visit to Dublin, she emphasised that her goal in 1995 was to win a medal at the European Championships for Ireland, and despite the lucrative temptations of the Dutch Olympic Council, there was still no question of her changing her national allegiances. 'No way, I'm Irish and that's that, I couldn't swim for any other flag,' said the fluent Irish speaker.

Vienna and the European Swimming Championships loomed in August and so Smith decided to rest from major competition until then. She continued to train in fifty metres on a daily basis and to improve her sprinting. For the first time since Gary O'Toole's silver medal in the European Championships, there seemed to be a real prospect of another and maybe even a gold. Certainly the 200 metres butterfly, for which Michelle was ranked number one in the world, seemed to be the one to watch out for.

In fact, the booty was delivered earlier than expected. Smith clocked up the fastest qualifying time for the heats in the 400 metres Individual Medley. That evening, she set to battle with the Olympic Champion Krisztina Egerszegi of Hungary. Smith raced ahead for the first two lengths of butterfly but the Champion came back. Egerszegi shot ahead during the backstroke, Smith clawed back in the breaststroke and freestyle but was just two seconds short at the wall. Silver, and Ireland's best ever swimming result was equalled.

But the best was yet to come.

Smith came agonisingly close in the 100 metres butterfly on the Friday. A tactical error placed her fifth in the final, just milliseconds behind the medals. The next day was the 200 metres individual medley and Smith deliberated whether to compete or not, just 24 hours before her own specialty; the 200 metres butterfly.

'Encouraged by Erik, I managed to distance myself from Friday's disappointment. My whole attitude changed when I was the fastest qualifier in the heats. Had I been eighth fastest, then yes, I would have withdrawn from the final.'

She made the right decision, and against the odds beat her rival Brigitte Bescue of Belgium to take the gold with the second fastest time in the world this year.

'I was never so focussed for a race. No looking about, tunnel vision all the way. Erik told me, "think only of your own swim, the electronic scoreboard will tell you how good you were". Funnily, my concentration was so intense that I almost forgot to look up to see my time after touching the finishing pads.'

Silver and gold in the swim bag, and her best event yet to come; the 200 metres butterfly.

Far from having produced her best already, Smith stormed to a lead and won the gold with wake to spare between her and her nearest rival Matte

Jacobsen of Denmark. She set a world-record pace early on, her tired limbs just fading over the last fifty metres.

'At the end I felt that the six races I had during the week were taking their toll all at once. It may have appeared that the pressure was off me going into the final today, but so many people were expecting me to do well in the 200 that I reacted.'

Back home in Rathcoole, the local support gathered in The Poiton Still pub to cheer on their girl. Through a complication of bookings, Michelle's father and mother, Brian and Pat, missed out on Vienna and watched from the bar. 'It's the culmination of our dreams, I'm so proud of her,' said Pat. 'I was delighted with the result but not surprised,' said Brian, who admitted later that he cried as he watched his daughter touch the wall in first place.

A telegram was despatched to Vienna from Áras an Uachtaráin, another congratulatory message for an Irish woman who had successfully chased the gold.

'Congratulations on your magnificent victories in the European Swimming Championships. Your success is a tribute to your dedication and courage and is well deserved.'

Later, former European silver medallist Gary O'Toole emphasised just how remarkable Michelle Smith's achievement had been in Vienna. She had entered no less than *four* events, swam world-class times in all heats and finals, and came away with three medals; one silver and two gold. And unbelievably,

Below: Michelle Smith with her gold medal for the 200 metres butterfly in the European Swimming Championships in Vienna, 1995.

she was kicking herself that she had thrown away the chance to win the gold in the 100 metres butterfly.

Smith's true grit and tenacity was exemplified by her performances in Vienna. It is little wonder then, that she is called 'Die Beste', or 'The Animal' back in her Dutch base of Dordrecht.

Like Sonia O'Sullivan, the Rathcoole woman watched the Chinese come from virtually nowhere and simply said to herself, I've got to work harder, rather than sit around and complain. Neither Irish woman likes to blow her own trumpet or sit on top of open-top buses taking the glory. They both prefer to get on with the job in hand — winning.

Michelle's next target is the Olympic Games at Atlanta and again like Sonia O'Sullivan, she knows that Vienna was just a dress rehearsal. The big one is yet to come, and this time she doesn't want to carry the flag, she wants to watch them raise it.

She'll keep going, too. As she says herself, 'I'll keep swimming anyway because I love it and it's what I want to do'.

Above: Racing for gold in the European Swimming Championships, 1995.

Sandra O'Gorman

Sandra O'Gorman has the unenviable task of being goalkeeper for Ireland's women's hockey team. A Dubliner from the suburb of Kilmacud, she started playing hockey at school for Muckross. Despite being eligible to play for Germany through her mother Elizabeth's native birthright, Sandra has established herself as Ireland's and indeed the world's leading goalkeeper in women's hockey. Sandra spent some time at college in the US on a hockey scholarship, and she has also coached full time at tennis. She is currently employed as a sales representative by a publishing company, while continuing to play hockey at the highest level.

~

My mother always says to me, "you could have played for Germany," but I always say to her, "I'm not German, Mom, I'm Irish".

If Sandra had declared for Germany, as she could have, chances are she would be their national women's hockey goalkeeper, and she would be looking forward to the Olympic qualification tournament in South Africa in 1995 and probably the Atlanta Olympics in 1996.

That is not the case, however. Sandra O'Gorman is the Irish women's hockey goalkeeper. Because Ireland lost to England in the Women's Hockey World Cup in Dublin in 1994, she and her teammates did not qualify for the South African tournament, and Atlanta became a forgotten dream.

Sandra could have qualified for Germany by virtue of her mother Elizabeth's birthright. Yet Elizabeth O'Gorman supported her daughter all the way through the 1994 Women's Hockey World Cup, as she has always done. At the end of her Muckross club matches, Elizabeth is there, ready to congratulate or commiserate, to supply whatever support is required — 'I guess she is my number one fan.'

In March 1994 the Irish women's team beat India 1-0 as part of their mini-tournament in advance of the Women's Hockey World Cup. Sandra had kept another clean sheet, and though coach Terry Gregg was not one to underestimate the very high standard of international hockey, he knew the team had the makings of a world-class goalkeeper in Sandra O'Gorman. She rose to the occasion of the Women's Hockey World Cup to play some of the best matches of her life, and to be awarded the trophy for Goalkeeper of the Tournament, an effective declaration that Sandra O'Gorman was the best in the world. 'Nobody can take that away from me. For the next four years, that is until the next Hockey World Cup, I'm the best goalkeeper in the world and that's the biggest award that can ever be given to a hockey player,' she says.

Some may think that Sandra O'Gorman blows her own trumpet, but she

Left: Sandra O'Gorman,
goalkeeper, Ireland.

knows that if she doesn't do it, nobody will. It takes courage, a great deal of courage, to be a goalkeeper in hockey, so it is hardly surprising that this quality translates to her everyday life. Imagine standing in a small, boxed-off area, with people hitting fist-sized hard round objects at you at point blank range.

That's what being a goalkeeper in hockey is all about. The object of the exercise is to get yourself between the goal and the ball, and even if the ball is travelling at sixty miles an hour, it must be stopped. Goalkeepers in other sports, particularly soccer, are constantly praised for their heroic saves. Add in the sheer element of danger and the narrowing of range, and the courage of hockey goalkeepers becomes all the more apparent.

In that case, why play in goals? Why not let somebody else get the injuries or the blame?

Sandra admits that she had no real desire to play the position. She doesn't know how it happened, but at the Dominican Convent of Muckross College in Donnybrook, county Dublin, Sandra somehow stayed in goals for the pea-green uniforms of her school until completing her Leaving Certificate in 1985. Then she was invited to attend university in the United States on a hockey scholarship.

She had a very good time in the US, but the competition there was mostly intervarsity and almost all on grass. Though many Irish athletes have taken up athletics, basketball and swimming scholarships in the US, hockey scholarships there have not been common. But a college in Providence, Rhode Island, contacted the ILHU, saying that they might have an opportunity for a hockey striker. There was no striker interested at the time, and when Sandra heard about it she decided to write to them. 'I suppose I told them I couldn't strike, but I could save, so I guess it did the trick,' she laughs.

Sandra, who was still studying for her Leaving Certificate in Muckross, wrote to the authorities in Providence, and outlined her sporting qualifications: under-eighteen Irish international tennis player and goalkeeper for the Irish schoolgirls' hockey team.

Sandra had to sit her SAT American college entrance exams before doing her Leaving Cert. With all academic trials behind her, she travelled to Providence College and embarked on a four-year degree in liberal arts.

The college is very academically driven, and she could only make the team after she had passed her exams. Hockey and tennis were her sporting occupations at Providence, and it not just in the role of hockey goalkeeper. She played a lot of outfield hockey and stayed on at the college after she had got her degree to work as assistant coach to the hockey team.

While at Providence, Sandra was named in the squad of the top sixteen college hockey players in the United States. She was also voted Athlete of the Year at Providence three years in a row.

Such sporting experience has undoubtedly helped her game enormously. Women's hockey has developed considerably as a game, and gone are the days when a goalkeeper would merely stay in her own target area. Since the abolition of the 'bully-off' and the lifting of restrictions on raising the stick, the game has become much more fluid, with plenty of passing, rather than the popular solo running of before. Playing hockey on modern astroturf sand- and water-based pitches has also influenced these tactical changes.

Likewise, goalkeepers are much more involved in the game, and they often act as a sweeper, coming out to the edge of the circle with their defence dropping behind them. Modern goalkeepers must have good mobility and good outfield ball skills. Of course, they must also have courage, eye-to-ball speed and co-ordination, especially when called upon to save. Goalkeepers have to be extremely fit and mobile now and are expected to come out and play a lot more. Sandra is the first line of defence. She acts as a sweeper more often than not, and only has to make saves some of the time.

As she has been playing hockey since she was twelve, Sandra's game has adapted with the changes and developments that have taken place in the sport. Consistently playing for Muckross A teams all the way through school, and then continuing with the club afterwards has helped tremendously.

After five successful years at Providence, O'Gorman returned to Ireland in 1990 because of commitments at home. She had been on a student visa while at college and while coaching, but then the university didn't seem that keen to sponsor her for a full visa so she came home. At the time she was engaged to be married, but after breaking up with her fiancé she decided to remain in Ireland rather than return to the US. It was then that her association with tennis resumed, and she worked as a coach with Harry Henry in Dun Laoghaire, county Dublin, for most of 1990, while starting to play with Muckross hockey club.

In 1991 the call came from the Irish team, and Sandra made her debut in goal against Germany, her mother's birthplace. It was a nightmare. She let in four goals, and Ireland lost the match, a European Championship game in Holland, by four goals to one. Ironically, her mother Elizabeth was visiting Germany at the time, and could have seen her daughter on television, at the wrong end of some fluent German play.

After three years' involvement with the Irish team, Sandra, Teresa Hurley and Mary Logue felt like the veterans of the squad during the 1994 hockey World Cup. Terry Gregg had gathered a very young team around him, and even captain Sarah Kelleher was only twenty-two. As elected hosts, Ireland was one of the twelve participating nations in the tournament. They knew they were going to be the underdogs in the tournament, so Terry Gregg was determined that his young squad would have the best preparation posssible.

Muckross and the other clubs agreed to play the season early so that the international players would be released in time to prepare together as a squad. They had regular squad sessions, and then friendly international matches, which were all a great help also. Gregg's training methods, which he brought from his club Lisnagarvey (the most successful men's hockey club in Ireland), brought the squad to a new high level of fitness, benefiting them and their clubs, many of whom adopted his approach. Muckross had its most successful year ever in 1994, winning the big three — the Leinster Senior League, the Leinster Senior Cup, and the Sharwoods All-Ireland Senior Cup.

The last of these was the sweetest, and one goal against Portadown made history for the Dublin club. After the final hooter in the match, O'Gorman raised her arms aloft and then ran over to embrace her mother on the sideline. A few weeks later, Sandra was back again at the Three Rock Rovers Club, playing for Ireland. They had just beaten India for the second time in a few days, and the two wins over the country ranked twelfth in the world gave the Irish women a good feeling of confidence.

The Irish team were conscious of being regarded as the hosts only. They did not want to be regarded as an also-ran country in the tournament only because of the host role. But the team's professional attitude and Gregg's excellent training earned them respect. For the first few months of 1994, the team ate, slept and dreamt their World Cup dream, while most of them kept down full-time jobs. Sandra O'Gorman continued her work as a sales representative with the Westwood Sports and Leisure Club in Leopardstown, county Dublin. She, like her teammates, added a few extra routines to her day;

longer runs and stretching and sprinting and a few better habits like a low-fat and high-energy diet. There was also the matter of cigarettes and alcohol. Sandra doesn't drink and never has, but she does enjoy the odd cigarette. That had to stop.

The same applied during the hockey World Cup itself. While thousands of visitors to the site at Belfield enjoyed the tented village and hospitality area, complete with live entertainment, the Irish team were packed back to their hotel every evening for a hearty meal and an early night. Such is dedication.

By the time the World Cup was about to start, the Irish team played their last friendly match on the newly-opened water-based pitch at Belfield. A good crowd turned out to wish the home team well and have a look at the new facilities, and they were awarded with a well-played draw.

And so to the World Cup itself.

Ireland were up against it from the start, as they were drawn in a fairly tough group with Argentina, Australia, Korea, Spain and Russia. Argentina were the first hurdle, and unfortunately for the home side, the South Americans were in sparkling form, particularly the brilliant Karina Masotta. Three goals clunked into the Irish goal, and the high standards of international hockey made themselves very obvious indeed. By general consensus, Caroline Craig, Sarah Kelleher and Sandra O'Gorman were Ireland's best players.

Next came Spain, and beforehand Terry Gregg set out what his team had to achieve, with a reminder of the facts of life. To get a point or a win, he knew they would have to play to the best of their ability and hope that their opponents were below their top form. The Olympic champions played well, but the Irish held them until nine minutes from the end. Then, to everyone's joy, a brilliant Sarah Kelleher goal from a penalty corner gave the Irish the lead. Could a win be on the cards? It seemed so until five minutes from the end, when Lucia Lupez scuttled through the Irish defence and scored the equaliser. A draw against the Olympic champions was certainly something to cherish, but a win had been snatched from their grasp. There was happiness tinged with disappointment, and Gregg noted that a win over Korea was now possible as the Koreans had lost to Spain earlier in the week.

Sadly that was not the case, and the Koreans' strength won out by two goals to nil. Again, seven saves from O'Gorman limited the damage, and it was generally accepted that Ireland were unlucky to lose as they had in fact played very well.

Next were Australia, daunting at the best of times. They had already shown they were in sparkling form. Four goals by the rampant Australians demonstrated the gulf in standards between the antipodes and the home team. However, if it wasn't for a certain O'Gorman, it could have been an awful lot worse. Her exceptional goalkeeping ensured that Ireland didn't lose by double figures. The Australians ran the legs off the Irish team, and if it wasn't for a succession of incredible O'Gorman saves, particularly in the second half when

Left: Saving a penalty stroke, Ireland v England, UCD, 1994.
Below: Diving the right way in the eighth Women's Hockey World Cup, 1994.

her goal was virtually peppered with shots, it could have been a cricket score. It got to the point that the Australians and the crowd wondered what had to be done to infiltrate the Irish goalmouth, with this headbanded fiend in front of it. Ireland may have lost, but O'Gorman had certainly made her mark on a global scale. Sixteen dramatic saves and only four goals conceded.

Next came Russia, with hopes of a win spurred on by 3,000 partisan supporters. A nil-all draw was the result, however, and the team now knew that a playoff for the last place in the pre-Olympic qualification tournament was on the cards. The only question was who the opposition would be, Canada or England.

At this point, both the team and coach were moved by the force of support for Ireland from the home crowds. Before the Belfield World Cup, the biggest crowd that they had played before was no more than a hundred or two, so several thousand roaring home fans bedecked in tricolours and painted faces was new territory. It also made the team want to give something back.

After England's three-nil defeat of Canada (their first win of the tournament), the perfect match was set up for the home crowd. A playoff for the South African tournament and a meeting with the old rivals, England.

The English team was made up of most of the same players who represented Great Britain at the 1992 Barcelona Olympics and who were the eventual bronze medallists. The last time Ireland had met them, they had drawn, and they were determined to go one better than that. Of course there was extra incentive; the losers would not go to South Africa, and would forfeit any chance they had of competing at the Atlanta Olympic Games in 1996.

As if that was not enough, the comments of English manager Jenny Cardwell after their win over Canada enraged the Irish team, and Terry Gregg made no secret of his annoyance with her. According to Cardwell, Ireland had only two players, captain and goalkeeper, and they would not cause the English too much of a problem. On Saturday, July 23, the battle raged. Boosted by the boisterous support of a few thousand supporters, the Irish team held the English up to a point, but with the distinctive red head of Sixsmith hovering dangerously around the circle, a blow for the visiting team was inevitable. A penalty corner from Sixsmith was connected with by Jill Aitken, and it was one-nil to England.

Although the Irish seemed somewhat dazed by the score, they renewed their pressure play, and Lynsey McVicker slotted home an equaliser from Judith Chapman's pass following a free just outside the circle, sending the packed crowd into ecstasies and chants of 'You'll Never Beat the Irish'. And they were nearly right. The second half produced some fine hockey, with both teams going all out for a win. It was, however, the heroics of O'Gorman in goal which kept the Irish in it.

Two dramatic saves from shots by Atkins and Johnson kept the Irish hopes alive, but just as she breathed a slight sigh of relief, O'Gorman was to be tested again. Judith Chapman was judged to have deliberately kicked the ball in the circle, and the resulting harsh decision by the umpires awarded a penalty flick to England. The crowd held their breath, and O'Gorman steeled herself on the line, slightly crouched, her face hidden behind her metal visor.

The stick moved swiftly, the ball flew, but O'Gorman's glove shot into the air and interrupted the flight of the hockey ball. Saved! The Irish team celebrated and resumed the task. Two missed chances for Ireland in the second half will live to haunt them for quite a long time, but they were nothing on what was to follow. Time ran out, the hooter sounded, and O'Gorman's greatest ever test loomed — penalty flicks.

This time she stood crouched in the other goal, with the home crowd bustling down around her, tense with anticipation. The Irish team stood in the centre of the pitch, just outside their dugout, in a state of nervous frenzy. Kathy Johnston walked up to take the stroke for England. O'Gorman crouched, and pounced. Thwack. Saved! Her third penalty save of the match, and all the Irish had to do now was score their own.

O'Gorman's joy as she stood in her padding, purple headband and warpainted cheeks, was sadly premature, as strange fates awaited the Irish team. Somehow, Sarah Kelleher, the Irish captain and one of the best players in the World Cup, managed to miss the goal completely. Nobody could believe it, and certainly not Sarah herself. The distinctive blonde head looked up in horror and she turned to walk away slowly.

Three weakly hit shots and another astonishing miss by Mary Logue put the lid on the Irish loss. As the English danced a shimmy around the middle of the pitch, the Irish hugged each other, devastated. It wasn't just a loss. The rung on the ladder to higher things and Olympic qualification was now gone.

Terry Gregg in particular was devastated by the loss. He also made it clear that he and the team had been far from happy with the attitude of the English team to the Irish before the match. Though the Irish proved the attitude wrong, it was not enough, and missing out on Olympic qualification was a heavy blow. Unfortunately, losing to England meant that Ireland had to play again the following morning against Russia, to avoid the wooden spoon.

After another night of abstinence (despite the tempation to drown their sorrows), the team assembled. Amazingly, a healthy crowd also turned out to support the Irish, no doubt filled with patriotic fervour by the exploits of the previous day. A three-two victory with goals from Jeanette Turner, Judith Chapman and Lynsey McVicker sealed the victory and eleventh place. It was also another impressive performance by O'Gorman, who saved six of eight shots on goal.

Yet Gregg and the team were disappointed. They had come to the tournament looking to finish ninth. They knew they had not fulfilled their potential, and they were not going to pretend that they were happy with less.

Later that afternoon, Australia defeated Argentina in a fairly disappointing final. The United States won a popular victory to finish third, and then it was all over bar the shouting. One hope for the Irish remained, however, the award for Goalkeeper of the Tournament.

As the teams lined up behind their flags, Elizabeth O'Gorman ran back into the arena to see the presentation of medals and trophies. All week she had spent her time commuting from the pitch to the tented village where she helped to sell the many thousands of World Cup souvenir items. But the best momento was yet to come.

As Roy Willoughby announced that Argentina's Karina Masotta had won Player of the Tournament, the crowd buzzed with anticipation. The award for goalkeeper of the tournament was next.

The teams were lined up and, as Sandra's name was announced, her arms shot into the air. This time you could see her face. As she came forward to collect her Waterford Crystal award, the crowd went apoplectic with joy. This is what they had been waiting for; an Irish victory and the best goalkeeper in the world.

Irish captain Sarah Kelleher moved to Dublin after the tournament and joined Muckross hockey club. There she was reunited with Mary Logue, Teresa Hurley and Sandra O'Gorman. But for the players, there were difficulties to face in the aftermath. The return to amateur status means the return to work and everyday life. However, life goes on. In March 1995, the Irish women's hockey team travelled to St Petersburg, the first time an Irish women's team had been invited to play there. It was an indication of the nation's new-found standing as one of the world's most respected hockey teams. And, after all, they do have the world's best goalkeeper.

'In a sporting sense, it is very interesting in that we have noticed that the guys in the hockey clubs seem to take us a lot more seriously now. Also, I think a lot of the old image of butch lesbian hockey players has been dismissed. It's like we have proved ourselves on an international stage so now they can respect us a lot more,' says O'Gorman.

'Also we've received more invitations to travel and play abroad and that's how you improve your game. I guess they are taking us a little more seriously around the world as well.

'On the minus side, after all the hype of the World Cup and all the media interest, nobody really wants to know us now, and I guess it'll be a few paragraphs of coverage in the newspapers of the club finals, but that's the way it goes, I suppose. Hockey is, after all, a "minority women's sport".'

The 1994 Women's Hockey World Cup

'I remember standing on the balcony of the sports centre of UCD on the first Saturday of the tournament and looking down on the pitch, and I nearly pinched myself because I didn't believe it was happening. And then I decided that I didn't have a worry in the world because it was all being looked after.' *Joan Priestman, Chairperson of the Women's Hockey World Cup, December 1994.*

In 1991 the Irish Ladies Hockey Union applied to the Federation Internationale de Hockey to host the 1994 Women's Hockey World Cup in Dublin. The ILHU tied in their application with the fact that the Irish organisation would be celebrating its centenary in the same year. The FIH voted on the matter, and Ireland was awarded the eighth Women's Hockey World Cup. Then the fun began.

Hosting the tournament cost about two million pounds, including the cost of building a specialised pitch. International standards demanded a state-of-the-art water-based pitch for all matches in the tournament. Ireland did not have one, and it would have to be built.

From the start, the ILHU were up against the odds. Not only would the event be enormously expensive, it also had to compete with the other world cup — USA '94, when soccer fans all over the globe would be glued to their television sets. Sponsorship and patronage had to be high on the agenda. On November 16, 1993, when an Alan McLoughlin goal ensured that the Republic of Ireland football team would be going to the USA, the task ahead of the ILHU's organising team looked an awful lot tougher.

From the start, the organising committee accepted that they would have to embark on an enormous fundraising scheme; not all finance would come from sponsorship or patronage. The ILHU set up a company to control all aspects of the organising of the tournament, from finance and fundraising to the running of the supporters' club. All had to be managed with hands-on efficiency.

The organising committee comprised chairperson Joan Priestman, honorary secretary Anita Manning, and honorary treasurer Rionach Donlon. There were eight sub-committees to deal with every aspect of the work, and the chairpersons of those committees also sat on a central committee.

The sub-committees looked after finance and fundraising, marketing and communications, venue and facilities, merchandise, travel and accommodation, ceremonies and functions, support services, and supporters clubs.

The organising committee knew it had to establish a financial base. It needed money and needed it fast, and so the great hockey draw was born. The official Women's Hockey World Cup draw was a monthly raffle, for which there were only a limited number of tickets. The key to its fundraising success was that the tickets were limited and expensive, as were the prizes. Every month, a car could be won, along with tickets to some of the premium sports events in the world like Wimbledon or the French Open. The ILHU knew that it had to raise a large amount of money itself, and that was the most effective way to do it.

Each ticket cost £100, entitling the entrant to participate in the draw every month for a year. Only 5,000 tickets were issued and all were sold, raising a profit of £250,000. A levy was then placed on every women's hockey club in Ireland, raising approximately £50,000.

The Irish government agreed to fund the tournament to the tune of £100,000, plus the building of the water-based pitch at UCD Belfield at a cost of £70,000. The site would include a permanent stand to accommodate 2,000 spectators. The site would be fully floodlit and situated to the rear of the UCD Sports Centre.

It made sense for the government to agree to this funding. The pitch would be another top-class sporting facility for Ireland, and its use for two major international hockey tournaments was already guaranteed; the Women's World Cup, and the Men's European Championships, which were hosted by Dublin in 1995.

The money gradually came in, but it was far from a picnic. Well into 1994 it looked likely that the ILHU would have to cope with a debt of over £150,000. In the meantime, Joan Priestman and her team made approaches and presentations to every major company in Ireland, and they concentrated particularly on those with an international profile. The tournament would be viewed in at least the twelve participating countries, if not others: Argentina, Canada, Australia, China, Ireland, England, Korea, Germany, Russia, the Netherlands, Spain and the US.

Dr Tony O'Reilly and Independent Newpapers stepped into the breach in May 1994 with a donation of £50,000 towards the running of the tournament. Irene Johnston welcomed the news with the immortal line, 'Never have you satisfied so many women in one day'.

The following Tuesday, less than two months before the World Cup was set to begin, Waterford Crystal came up with the title sponsorship, which was worth over £120,000 between money and crystal trophies, the latter for presentation and purchase.

The tournament needed RTE to film the matches and then provide a clean feed to each of the nations that requested the pictures. The ILHU had to pay RTE £54,000 for this service (which all agreed was excellently and expertly provided). They then had to await the returns from the individual international television stations to reimburse the cost. There was no guarantee that this

Sarah Kelleher **(above)** and **(below)** Teresa Hurley, Ireland v Korea in the Women's World Cup, 1994

would happen, as the international sports company IMG was handling the rights to the competition and did not regard the Women's Hockey World Cup as a top priority for selling worldwide. Fortunately, all the money paid to RTE was reimbursed through the payment of television rights through IMG to the ILHU, and by the end of 1994 the full amount had been recovered.

The Waterford Crystal Women's Hockey World Cup began at UCD Belfield on July 13, 1994, as scheduled. Over forty thousand people visited the World Cup site and village over the eleven days that it ran, enjoying the hockey and the hospitality of the tented village. So successful was the selling of merchandise and souvenirs during the week of the tournament, the organisers began to realise that they might actually make a profit.

This was tremendous news for the ILHU, who had in six months gone from the threat of losing a lot of money, to making some, which would be pumped back into the sport in Ireland. The aim of hosting the Hockey World Cup after all, was not just to host a tremendous event in Ireland, but to develop the sport on a national level.

Four years of proper planning and the committed work of so many volunteers paid off. And it shouldn't be forgotten that God gave Ireland ten beautiful days in July something you cannot buy here.

Below: The Irish National Women's Hockey team at the official opening ceremony of the eighth Women's Hockey World Cup at Dublin Castle.

Health, Drugs and Sex

'I have picked up the pieces of so many Irish female athletes, I couldn't even say how many.'

Dr Maura O'Brien of Trinity College Dublin is not alone. The former medical officer to the Olympic Council of Ireland (OCI) and a member of the World Body of Sports Medicine is one of many Irish doctors who recognises the medical problems that female athletes face, in Ireland or elsewhere.

The same problems crop up: irregular and infrequent menstruation, stress fractures, osteoporosis, and dieting deseases like anorexia nervosa and bulimia. Athletes arrive into surgery with bones so brittle and osteoporosis so advanced, it is often too late to help. Female athletes are particularly prone. Many female middle-distance runners are hormonally deficient to the point that their menstrual cycles are highly irregular. In Ireland, quite a few female athletes who showed extaordinary talent in their teenage years have seen it all go untapped because they have fallen victim to stress fractures and eating disorders.

By virtue of their physiological make-up, women are susceptible to such problems. Athletes of a young age can suffer from overtraining, stress and deficient diet. Inappropriate training methods or too much training, combined with financial or social stress and a low-calorie diet, is a lethal cocktail. One of the first areas to be affected are the hormones, which means that the menstrual system suffers. Menstruation becomes irregular, and athletes begin to lose their periods altogether. This causes them to lose mineral density in their bones and then stress fractures start to appear. All of the above is exacerbated when the athlete is on a low-calorie diet, compounded by the myth that fitness is improved with low body fat. Athletes don't eat enough, and in some cases they become anorexic or bulimic.

To the uninitiated, such talk may seem alarmist, but only a few years ago it was widely believed that one of Ireland's international middle-distance runners was suffering from anorexia while still competing on the world stage. At least two promising Irish teenage athletes in recent years have become seriously ill with similiar eating disorders. One of these, a young woman in her teens with outstanding talent, spent months in hospital, and her weight dropped to under five stone. Only last year, a young American female athlete died of malnutrition.

'Athletes are not eating enough in the belief that it will improve their performance,' says Dr O'Brien. 'They should be cutting down on fats, but they must eat carbohydrates to compensate, and if they are training a lot they must have a lot of rest. Sleep is not just for the obvious rest effects. During sleep, the body secretes a growth hormone which is a naturally produced steroid. If the body is deprived of sleep, it loses out on these advantages.'

But the story is not all bleak. A few simple measures can be taken to monitor the body's performance and help the athlete avoid such problems. According to Dr O'Brien, the key to keeping well in the early days is to keep a training diary and monitor activity. Athletes should keep a close eye on training, diet, and their menstrual cycle. They should be physiologically examined regularly and monitored accordingly. It is important to remember that no two athletes are the same, and strict rules do not apply. Many of the women who run into trouble are those that have trained themselves, and also those who have come under pressure from parents and coaches.

Irish sports medicine has advanced enormously in recent years. A few years ago athletes like Mary Treacy had few options when it came to discussing their physiological development in relation to their performance as an athlete. Now there are many experts, including Drs Maura O'Brien, Geraldine Barnaville, Pat O'Neill and Joe Cumiskey, all professional in the field of sports medicine, and more and more medical students are opting for that area of research.

Sports injury clinics are now in operation in Trinity College Dublin, the Blackrock Clinic in Dublin, and at the University of Limerick. The most recent clinic to open is the one in University College Dublin at Belfield, which was established by sports administrator Dr Tony O'Neill. As UCD expands its programme of sports scholarships, so too must it develop the facilities to match. Increasingly, Irish athletes are opting for sports scholarships in Ireland and not in the US, but for the choice to be realistic, the facilities available here must be equivalent to those on offer abroad. Otherwise, the Irish institution is appealing to the athlete to stay only out of a sense of patronage.

Although facilities have improved beyond recognition, it is still clear that the emphasis is balanced in favour of those living in and around the Dublin area. There is still the option of Northern Ireland, where Queens University has another excellent facility. It is no coincidence that the Derry football team in 1992 used Queens in advance of the All-Ireland football final. In 1994 members of the Down football team travelled to the British national training centre in Lilleshall, Wales, for treatment.

At Trinity, Dr Maura O'Brien and her team monitor many athletes' progress and condition, and they have been very involved with Tennis Ireland. Karen Nugent and the Irish Ladies' Hockey Team have benefited from their attentions, but in particular the clinic at TCD has been closely involved with Catherina McKiernan's development as an athlete.

Catherina has been attending the Trinity centre since 1990, when she first started training seriously. Her coach, Joe Doonan, investigated the college's clinic, and they have had a symbiotic relationship with the Cavan athlete ever since. Catherina's presence has benefited the university's research. The first day she was there, the staff could tell that Catherina was oustanding in her aerobic capacity, and that it was obvious she was quite a talent, particularly suited to long-distance running.

However, Catherina was still only twenty and not yet developed enough for long-distance running. That is why she has paced her development, and has been monitored all the time.

Mistakes can be made. Seven years ago the centre took a group who were training for the Dublin City Marathon. They lost fifty per cent of that group in the first three months of training because of biomechanical problems — feet, ankles and hips siezing up. And all those who dropped out were young, from twenty to twenty-two years of age. At that age, athletes are physically capable of the distances in terms of heart and lungs, but not for the pounding, jarring and running.

In Trinity College, Dr Kelly and her team monitor the athletes on various apparatus, including the treadmill, the bicycle and the rowing machine. While the athlete is exercising, they measure the lactate buildup in the muscles (a sign of overtiredness or overtraining) and the heart rate. The athlete's bone density is measured on a 'DEXA', which is a holigic x-ray bone densitometer. In plain language, the machine measures the bone density in the athlete by using a form of x-ray, but with a much higher dosage. It is the only machine in the Republic of Ireland, though there is another in Queens University in Belfast. With this they can see immediately if an athlete is in trouble and can compare the results with the weight, height and heart rate of the individual, all of which are kept in computerised files. Like academic progress, the athlete's medical track record can be clearly monitored, and steps taken if something goes astray.

'Rest is so commonly overlooked, it is quite extraordinary. Over the years, the Sebastian Coes and Steve Ovetts of this world generally did not run in the indoor season in the United States, whereas Irish men did. Most of the time our athletes did this because of money, but many of them were probably overraced when they came to the big events,' says Dr O'Brien.

It is perhaps worth considering that Eamon Coghlan won his World Championship gold medal in Helsinki in 1983, after he had moved up a distance to the 5000 metres but also after he had greatly cut down on his race running. Many believe that Sonia O'Sullivan fell prey in 1994 to the temptation to overrace and overtrain. The impact of the Chinese athletes at the World Championships at Stuttgart in 1993 was considerable, and even though O'Sullivan claimed not to be bothered by them or their methods, she noticeably upped her training the following winter and was injured in the process. After a particularly hectic summer of racing in 1994, it was obvious to all observers that she was exhausted at the end of the season.

Sports psychology is another growing phenomenon in Ireland. Many athletes now talk of 'thinking through' the event before they run it and going over every possible or likely scenario in order that they be prepared for them. Before the Olympic final in Barcelona in 1992, Sonia O'Sullivan admitted that she was completely wound up with tension and that she could not eat or relax. In contrast, before her European Championships final in 1994 she said that she had thought through every possible outcome of the race and couldn't see herself not winning it. O'Sullivan also found time to rest on that day of the race to the point that she actually fell asleep.

The issue of drugs in sport is becoming more and more prevalent. Drugs are internationally used in sport, and the temptation to look to a performance-enhancing substance must be huge. Testing is on the increase, but the cost is prohibitive in a small country like Ireland. More and more sports organisations, however, are tuning into the culture of drug-free sport and moves by groups like the Irish Basketball Association and the GAA to carry out drug tests show that the issue is being taken very seriously.

Dr Joe Cumiskey of the Olympic Council of Ireland maintains that until an Irish athlete is tested as positive, we cannot be said to be doing the job of detection thoroughly enough here. He also likes to remind us that small though Ireland is, it is not the innocent territory that people like to think. Irish athletes are out there in the international arena and they have been out there for years. They are as susceptible as the next person to drug-taking and there are no sacred cows.

Athletes are becoming increasingly more aware of the list of banned substances circulated by the International Olympic Committee. Many everyday products which can be bought across the counter in chemists contain some of these, which is why athletes who are tested positive often mention that they were taking a cough syrup or decongestant. In some cases they are telling the truth, and in others it is a handy excuse. For women who suffer from acute menstrual pain, the option of taking codeine is out of the question. Sufferers usually opt for the contraceptive pill to reduce pain and the intensity of the menstruation. That has its own disadvantages, including mood change and weight gain, but these are the choices that must be made.

What is certain is that testing for drugs is going to become more and more a regular feature of sport.

Gender testing is as common a feature in sport in recent years, although many believe that with the advents of the successful Chinese athletes it could make a comeback. The first woman to undergo a gender test at an Olympic Games, incidentally, was Belfast's own Mary Peters.

It is impossible to compare truly the performance of women and men in sport. What is true is that despite the considerable physiological differences, women have caught up with their male counterparts in sport. Obviously, this improvement only goes so far, but considering that a hundred years ago women were banned from participating in the Olympic Games, things have changed considerably.

Money, Money, Money

The commercial world of Irish sport has developed enormously over the last few decades. Sport in Ireland still relies to a great extent on the goodwill of thousands of volunteers, but adequate finance is usually the most valued commodity.

In Ireland there are many causes and requests for sponsorship, and unfortunately the bowl is small. It is a fact of life that some will hit the target and others simply will not. Women's sport in Ireland is still considered by the media and prospective sponsors as a minority sport. Obviously women are not a physical minority in Ireland, but the truth is that due to the relatively low coverage of women's sport in the media — print, audio or televisual — it is perceived as a minority interest. Research of all of media by the Council for the Status of Women in 1992 showed this to be the case.

Some in the business estimate that women get only ten per cent of coverage in the media. The situation is not to be desired, and it will not change today, but there are movements in the right direction. Complaining may not bring about change in the establishment, but constructive action will.

Many sporting bodies that embark on campaigns to get sponsorship come up against the same line — what's in it for me, and what coverage will I get? Sports that traditionally have little coverage cannot expect a sponsor to come bounding along with open arms. But there are relatively easy ways to overcome this problem. And it is worth noting that the same problems beset men's sport.

The media is by its nature a relatively lazy beast. If an item is served up to them and it is interesting enough to merit attention it should get it. However, that item should be served up well.

The following hints may be of help:

1. The item should have a hook or a point to it

Is one member of the team or club particularly successful or interesting? Is she a world champion, or six years of age, or a nun? Is she as successful at other sports? Pick out the points pithily and outline them clearly on a single sheet of paper. Try and arrange a catchy black-and-white photo to accompany the picture. If you are unknown, you have to make yourself interesting.

2. Address the release to the right person

It is startling how many press releases arrive at papers addressed to people who have emigrated or died. A simple phone call to the switchboard of the newspaper or station concerned can sort that out. Also, read the papers, and not just on one day. Look at who has weekly columns, for example. Send the release to them if you think it might suit their profile. Make yourself known to the *relevant* people.

3. Use your head

Do not annoy people with trivia or repeated phone calls. And do not expect fifty-two reporters to turn up to your press conference. If they don't know you and if it's not the launch of the Irish bid for the Olympics, generally speaking people will not turn up. It is not out of arrogance or rudeness; there quite simply isn't the time. Faxed releases and delivered photos accompanied by a phone call are the simplest way of having a press launch covered.

4. The direct letter

Possible features usually merit a directed letter to the persons concerned. Why would this person want to write a feature on the subject? Put yourself in her shoes all the time. And remember, papers and stations are always looking for stories, but they must be stories. As Donal Foley once said, 'Dog bites man isn't news, but man bites dog, now that's news'.

4. Get to know times of publication

Morning and evening paper staffs do not usually meet, and neither do day and nightime staff in radio and television. Treat them as separate entities. Sunday papers are also completely separate, even if the titles are in the same group.

Such measures can greatly help a sport's case in getting coverage. The more you throw at the wall, but with precise direction and timing, the more you will achieve. And logically, the more proof of extra or increasing coverage you have, the better armed you are to go in search of sponsorship. It all comes down to the audience. You have to figure out if the event, person or team is compatible with what the company wants to do or wants to get at. You have to establish what you can give the sponsor, how many people you can give them access to through you or your event.

In sponsorship it all comes down to exposure. How many thousand people will be reached by sponsoring this event — and will they be the right kind of people? Match the event to the product. Look around and see who is sponsoring what; that is the easiest way of getting to know a company's profile.

Matching sponsorship opportunity with the right type of sponsor is crucial. And if you approach a company in a prepared and commercially aware manner, you will get a much more positive response; they might at least meet you. Just as newpapers abhor the long and boring press release, public relations companies dread the arrival of the stock sponsorship appeal letter. A generic letter is not only insulting to the prospective sponsor or agent, it suggests you have not researched your market.

Ironically, most people involved in public relations and communications companies recommend going straight to the person involved. It is simply easier to convince one person rather than two, but the key is to get to the right person and make the correct approach. Also, know whether you are seeking sonsorship, patronage, advertising or charity.

Sponsorship

This is when a company gets involved with an event or person, when there will be a tangible return for the investor. The event or person must be compatible with the company, and the sponsor can expect to increase its market share and its turnover as a result. It is often the case with sponsorship that the company initiates the project. Sponsorship is usually embarked on as a three-year deal, therefore guaranteeing a follow-up. A one-year event is unusual in sponsorship.

An example in women's sport: The TSB Women's Tennis Classic.

Patronage

This is when a company gets involved with a project where the two may be linked but a tangible result is not necessarily expected. Publicity and an increase in business should follow, but most are as a bonus rather than a necessity. Oftentimes there is a personal link between the patron and the event or project.

An example in women's sport:
The Waterford Crystal Women's Hockey World Cup.
(Harsh but true. Waterford Crystal and Independent Newspapers Ltd rescued the Women's Hockey World Cup due to the intervention of Dr AJF O'Reilly. The event was always going to go ahead, but it looked likely that the ILHU were going to be saddled with a large debt, but for the patronage of Dr O'Reilly and two of his companies.)

Advertising

This is when a company is approached to buy space or time at an event, or on an athlete's uniform. Advertising is usually done on a series basis and only occasionally as a once-off. Sponsors usually assume that advertising is part of the package; they expect the person or item to 'give' themselves for advertising opportunities.

An example in women's sport: West Coast Cooler Meteors basketball team.

Charity

This is when a worthy cause is supported by a company. It is usually something of benefit to the social fabric of society. As a rule, a company should never expect to get a commercial return from charity.

For women looking for sponsorship a few unwritten rules apply. If the sport or area does not traditionally attract a lot of publicity in the media, there must be another hook. Sponsors want 'safe women'. They don't want risky women, the people in the business say, and they don't want gay women. Chris Evert and Gabriella Sabatini never had a problem getting a sponsor, but Martina Navratilova did. They usually want young, personable well-known women. Sponsors want famous people, and the basis for that, whether people like it or not, is television. If you have been on either *The Late Late Show* or *The Pat Kenny Show* and another mainstream programme, people regard you as famous.

Women who want sponsorship have to be prepared to play the game. As Rosemary Smith says, 'When a sponsor says jump, I say how high?'

If an athlete is sponsored by a food company, she must be prepared to get into the kitchen and smile. You have no permission ever to be off-colour or premenstrual; you can't spoil the image. You have to be perfect to be a sponsor's dream.

In these times of economic belt-tightening, the sponsorship bowl is getting ever smaller. It is a battle between many worthy causes to see who is going to get the deal, and if you don't have the contacts you are starting off with a handicap. The solution is simple and far more easily attainable than many people think; if you don't have the contacts, work on what you do have, make introductions and make those connections.

In December 1994, the first-ever National Forum for Women's Sport in Ireland was held in Dublin Castle. The one-day conference, which included many workshops and think-ins, was in effect a think-tank for the hundreds of people involved in women's sport around Ireland.

But perhaps no greater promotion for sport itself has been done by the people who are on top of the world and representing Ireland.

Those people, who in the 1920s were horrified at the spectacle of women cavorting before the public gaze, would be amazed that such great achievements would be made by women, and perhaps even more so that the congratulations telegrams of 1995 were signed by An tUachtarán, Mrs Mary Robinson.

To Sonia O'Sullivan:

'Your magnificient achievement is a cause for pride and celebration throughout Ireland and a great personal triumph in your aspiring athletic career.' President Mary Robinson.

WANDERING WOMEN
Two Centuries of Travel Out of Ireland
A. A. Kelly

Spanning the five continents, Wandering Women presents travel writings from the 1790s to the 1990s. These thirty-seven intrepid travellers include Anna Jane Thornton who posed as a male sailor in order to get to New York, Beatrice Grimshaw, world-record cyclist who is still remembered in Papua and Daisy Bates who recorded the lives of the Australian Aborigines.

These are tales drawn from journals, autobiographies, letters and private diaries as well as the travel books of present day professionals such as Dervla Murphy. These women write as wives or companions, as political exiles, emigrants, nuns, journalists, servants or anthropologists. Across Russia, Canada and the Atlantic ocean to the USA, the Pacific islands, Africa and Tibet, they travel by canoe and camel, ox-wagon and bicycle. Some are solo explorers, some travel on duty, for pleasure or for economic gain. Most are adventurous, some foolhardy but all write in vivid and memorable ways.

PB £11.99 B/W photos 240pp **ISBN** 0 86327 445 5

HURLING GIANTS
Brendan Fullam

As you open the pages, you will hear again the roar of the crowds in Croke Park, the whirr of the flying sliotar and the unmistakable and unique sound of ash against ash. — (Review of Giants of the Ash)

Hurling Giants is a classic from the author of the greatest hurling book of all time. Packed with interviews, photographs, team choices, autographs, statistics and text by the players themselves, this book captures and celebrates views, memories and achievement from this game of speed and skill.

This completely new selection includes: modern masters of the game, the great camogie players, giants of former years, and special profiles of the game's five 'Giants among Giants'.

HB £15.99 Colour and B/W photos 276pp **ISBN** 0 8637 444 7

THE CHAMPIONSHIP 1995
Football & Hurling
The Complete Record

Brian Carthy

1995 has proved to be a dramatic year in Gaelic games with two dynamic championship series — the hurling series crowned by the sight of Anthony Daly lofting the McCarthy before an ecstatic cheering crowd of fellow Clare people, the county's first victory in the All-Ireland in over 80 years; and in football, perhaps not surprisingly yet another northern team reaches the final after a tripple run from Donegal, Derry and Down to challenge a renewed set of Dubs in a great final.

The Championship by Brian Carthy is the complete record from the first game of the year to the two finals, and all the excitement and sportsmanship in between. It contains team photos, full team listings, match details and reports, as well as features articles on great and new players such as Jason Sherlock, Charlie Redmond, D. J. Carey, the Dooleys, and the managers of the victorious teams.

For all sports followers this is the complete picture, illustrated in black and white and colour. Brian Carthy is the author of the classic *Football Captains* (also from Wolfhound Press) and works as sports reporter and a leading GAA commentator with RTE.

PB Illustrated 224pp Available October 1995 **ISBN** 0 86327 516 8

These books are available from all good bookshops or direct from
WOLFHOUND PRESS,
68 Mountjoy Square,
Dublin 1.
Tel: 8740354 Fax: 8720207.
Call or write for our full catalogue.